Computer Technology

Other books in the Careers for the Twenty-First Century series:

Aeronautics
Biotechnology
Education
Engineering
Law Enforcement
Medicine
Music
The News Media

Careers
for the
Twenty-First
Century

Computer
Technology

By Patrice Cassedy

**LUCENT
BOOKS®**

THOMSON

™

GALE

San Diego • Detroit • New York • San Francisco • Cleveland
New Haven, Conn. • Waterville, Maine • London • Munich

On Cover:

© 2004 by Lucent Books. Lucent Books is an imprint of The Gale Group, Inc.,
a division of Thomson Learning, Inc.

Lucent Books® and Thomson Learning™ are trademarks used herein under license.

For more information, contact
Lucent Books
27500 Drake Rd.
Farmington Hills, MI 48331-3535
Or you can visit our Internet site at www.gale.com

LIBRARY OF CONGRESS CATALOGING-IN-PUBLICATION DATA

Cassedy, Patrice.
    Computer technology / by Patrice Cassedy.
        p. cm. — (Careers for the 21st century)
    Summary: Discusses various positions available in the field of computer technology, discussing qualifications, training, and job opportunities.
        ISBN 1-56006-896-5 (hardback : alk. paper)
        1. Electronic data processing—Vocational guidance—Juvenile literature. 2. Computer science—Vocational guidance—Juvenile literature. [1. Data processing—Vocational guidance. 2. Computer science—Vocational guidance. 3. Vocational guidance.] I. Title. II. Series: Careers for the twenty-first century.
        QA76.25.C33 2004
        004'.023—dc22
                                                                            2003021391

Printed in the United States of America

Contents

Foreword

Young people in the twenty-first century are faced with a dizzying array of possibilities for careers as they become adults. However, the advances in technology and a world economy in which events in one nation increasingly affect events in other nations have made the job market extremely competitive. Young people entering the job market today must possess a combination of technological knowledge and an understanding of the cultural and socioeconomic factors that affect the working world. Don Tapscott, internationally known author and consultant on the effects of technology in business, government, and society, supports this idea, saying, "Yes, this country needs more technology graduates, as they fuel the digital economy. But . . . we have an equally strong need for those with a broader [humanities] background who can work in tandem with technical specialists, helping create and manage the [workplace] environment." To succeed in this job market young people today must enter it with a certain amount of specialized knowledge, preparation, and practical experience. In addition, they must possess the drive to update their job skills continually to match rapidly occurring technological, economic, and social changes.

Young people entering the twenty-first-century job market must carefully research and plan the education and training they will need to work in their chosen careers. High school graduates can no longer go straight into a job where they can hope to advance to positions of higher pay, better working conditions, and increased responsibility without first entering a training program, trade school, or college. For example, aircraft mechanics must attend schools that offer Federal Aviation Administration–accredited programs. These programs offer a broad-based curriculum that requires students to demonstrate an understanding of the basic principles of flight, aircraft function, and electronics. Students must also master computer technology used for diagnosing problems and show that they can apply what they learn toward routine maintenance and any number of needed repairs. With further education, an aircraft mechanic can gain increasingly specialized licenses that place him or her in the job market for positions of higher pay and greater responsibility.

In addition to technology skills, young people must understand how to communicate and work effectively with colleagues or clients from diverse backgrounds. James Billington, librarian of Congress, ascertains that "we do not have a global village, but rather a globe on which there are a whole lot of new villages . . . each trying to get its own place in the world, and anybody who's going to deal with this world is going to have to relate better to more of it." For example, flight attendants are increasingly being expected to know one or more foreign languages in order for them to better serve the needs of international passengers. Electrical engineers collaborating with a sister company in Russia on a project must be aware of cultural differences that could affect communication between the project members and, ultimately, the success of the project.

The Lucent Books Careers for the Twenty-First Century series discusses how these ideas come into play in such competitive career fields as aeronautics, biotechnology, computer technology, engineering, education, law enforcement, and medicine. Each title in the series discusses from five to seven different careers available in the respective field. The series provides a comprehensive view of what it's like to work in a particular job and what it takes to succeed in it. Each chapter encompasses a career's most recent trends in education and training, job responsibilities, the work environment and conditions, special challenges, earnings, and opportunities for advancement. Primary and secondary source quotes enliven the text. Sidebars expand on issues related to each career, including topics such as gender issues in the workplace, personal stories that demonstrate exceptional on-the-job experiences, and the latest technology and its potential for use in a particular career. Every volume includes an "Organizations to Contact" list as well as annotated bibliographies. Books in this series provide readers with pertinent information for deciding on a career and as a launching point for further research.

Introduction

A Definite Yet Unpredictable Future

Computers are so efficient at completing tasks that they are sometimes considered to be the machine equivalent of the human brain. However, author and expert computer programmer Jesse Liberty has this to say about computers: "The thing you need to know about computers is that, at bottom, they are really (really!) dumb. They don't know anything about letters, sentences, commands, numbers, buttons, windows, or the Internet. All computers know, at their deepest level, is electricity."[1] Thus, without the sophisticated efforts of many different workers, the computer would not be one of the most useful machine humans have ever known. According to the U.S. Census Bureau, Americans held more than 3 million jobs in the computer software and hardware industries in 1998. While it is nearly impossible in the twenty-first century for most Americans to go through a day without encountering and making good use of computer technology, most people do not stop to think about the effort that has been put into creating them. Americans take for granted flying safely from one city to another, "talking" online, receiving a host of website links after typing a word into a search engine, or playing a video game on a console or cell phone.

Just as Americans at the end of the twentieth century became complacent about computers, many assumed that jobs in computer fields would always be plentiful and lucrative. However, the 1990s through 2003 brought important shifts that make the future for Americans in computer fields unpredictable. The up-and-down economy of the 1990s, combined with the collapse of the dot-com industry, led to layoffs for thousands of computer workers. Another trend that is expected to alter the landscape for American workers in the computer industry is the outsourcing of jobs to other countries, especially India. Many American-based companies are moving their offices overseas and hiring local workers because it saves a significant amount of money on salaries.

The job outlook for computer careers is, therefore, hard to predict. In 2002 and 2003, the Bureau of Labor Statistics made these optimistic predictions for those in the field: From 2000 to 2010, network and systems administrators were predicted to see a 145 percent increase in the number of jobs; software engineers, 95 percent; and hardware engineers, 25 percent. Other sources, too, suggest that those in the field should remain hopeful about opportunities. At the same time, the *San Diego Union-Tribune*

The job outlook for computer professionals in the United States is uncertain. Many companies outsource jobs overseas, where people like this Indian engineer work for less money.

summarized statistics compiled by the U.S. Department of Labor and a well-known research company that suggest that between 2000 and 2015, the number of computer jobs outsourced to foreign countries could increase from about twenty-seven thousand to almost half a million. On Monster, the online career center, Allan Hoffman summarized the view of Dr. Howard Rubin, executive vice president of META, a firm that does research and consulting: "Most companies are not planning to recruit large numbers of [information technology] workers [in 2003] . . . and when they do move forward with [information technology] projects, they increasingly see global outsourcing as an option."[2]

Even before all of these changes, careers in computers required more flexibility than other careers, because technologies change rapidly, and companies, especially small ones, expected workers to shift from one area to another as the need arose. Commenting that Americans should improve the way students are prepared for careers in technology, Chris Stephenson and George Milbrandt write in *Learning and Leading with Technology*, "To work in the computer field, students must be prepared to accept constant change; openly investigate new programming languages, computer equipment, and application packages; and examine new ideas and procedures."[3]

This advice will ring true as the twenty-first century progresses. Excellence and flexibility will continue to be standards of the industry, but the bar will be raised. Employees with certification in more than one specialty; who have gained experience while attending associate, bachelor's or master's programs or in the workplace; and who are willing to relocate and devote themselves even more energetically to their jobs, will do best. Career consultant Kim R. Wells, who characterizes 2003 as one of the most competitive years for job seekers in many years because both new graduates and out-of-work veterans were in the market, gives this advice: "You will have to invest quality time in understanding the changing needs of employers, refining your job search strategies and tools, and ultimately deciding which prospective companies are a strong match for your talents and interests."[4]

Chapter 1

Computer Programmers

Computer programmers create programs, allowing users to make effective use of their computers. Programs are lines of instructions called "code" that tell the computer how to process information. Because machines—in this case, computers—do not speak the same language as their human users, programmers act, in effect, as translators, creating a means for the machine to understand human commands. Programmers use many different programming languages, but all languages have this in common: They require the programmer to develop lines of code and decide on the best sequence or order (logic) for those lines. Programmers' efforts may result in a workable operating system—the software that controls the basic functioning of a computer—or an application—the software that allows users to do specific tasks, such as word processing. One online writer described the critical work of programmers this way: "Every software package, operating system and application you can think of is the result of thousands of lines of code that were composed, entered and tested by a computer programmer."[5]

Programmers work in most types of companies, including banks, universities, and government agencies. Companies that employ the most programmers are those that create software or process data. Some programmers work independently, providing programming help for companies on an as-needed basis.

Planning Makes Perfect

Programmers begin their job by identifying the purpose of the program they have been assigned to write. This typically involves meetings with people who decide on or oversee the technological

11

Computer programmers develop a Sony Playstation game. Programmers work for many different types of companies and create a variety of different software.

needs of a company, such as systems analysts. The purpose may be to create a spreadsheet that allows company accountants to keep track of income and expenses. Or it may be to allow air traffic controllers to keep track of a host of airplanes and their locations relative to each other. Max Gardner, a software developer (programmer), explains how he approaches a program in the initial stages: "When I start writing a piece of software, I usually try to think about what I hope to accomplish: what problem I am solving, who will use it, who will be affected by it."[6]

Once programmers understand the purpose of the program, they develop a plan. This is necessary because programming is a complex task that can easily get out of control. This point is explained in C: *The Complete Reference* by programming expert Herbert Schildt: "Creating a large computer program is a little like designing a large building. There are so many bits and pieces that it almost seems impossible to make everything work together."[7]

Depending on the complexity of the project and how much experience a programmer has, the planning phase can be informal, consisting of a few notes. However, it is more typical for programmers to create diagrams and flow charts that show how the programming will proceed. Gardner explains how the complexity of the project and the work environment—whether he is on his own or part of a team—affects the planning process:

> When I am programming by myself, it's often enough to jump right in and begin programming after just sketching out the main ideas in my head. However, when I need to coordinate with a team of programmers, the process is much slower and more deliberate because we need to make group decisions on how different parts of the program will communicate. . . . [Once this is] agreed upon, each programmer can implement his or her own component however they wish. . . . In larger projects, it's especially important to discuss the problems with the entire programming team using diagrams and flow charts in order to help guide the overall structure of the software.[8]

Selecting and Using the Computer Language

Most programmers know more than one programming language, and they often make choices about the best language to use for a given project. Leon Atkinson, a computer expert who wrote a reference book on how to use the programming language PHP, uses a simple analogy to explain computer languages: "Instructions for baking a cake are called a recipe. Instructions for making a movie are called a screenplay. Instructions for a computer are called a program. Each of these is written in its own language, a concrete realization of an abstract set of instructions."[9]

A programmer's decision about which language to use for a project may be dictated by their employer's preference or the programmer's comfort level with one language over another. However, programmers often consider other factors. These include the speed and power they need for a specific project. Programmers learn over time which languages are best for solving which kinds of problems. For instance, to write a simple application in a hurry, a programmer may use Visual Basic. However, C++ is considered to be a more powerful language that gives programmers more control over how the computer behaves. Gardner illustrates these differences this way: "To compare, a small Windows program written in Visual Basic might take a few hours to write, whereas the same program would require several days in C++. However, the Visual Basic program might be much slower, more resource intensive, and more limited in its functionality than the C++ program."[10]

Languages range from low level (those written in language closest to computer language that need little or no additional translation by special software) to high level (those written in a language more understandable to humans but that need further translation by special software in order for the computer to interpret what the programmer has coded). The earliest and lowest-level language, machine language, is a system of binary numbers (0s and 1s).

A programmer's choice of language affects how they complete a programming project. C++ and Java are examples of high-level languages commonly used at the dawn of the twenty-first century. They are object-oriented languages. They differ from earlier languages (many of which are still used by programmers) that require the programmer to write a series of instructions, with each instruction leading logically to the next instruction. With object-oriented languages, programmers combine, manipulate, and reuse collections of instructions that are, in effect, packaged into little boxes, referred to as the objects. These objects act as building blocks. They help programmers in a couple of significant ways. First, they make programs more portable, meaning that a program can be used on different hardware or with different operating systems without a great deal of effort. They also preserve the programmer's work because they allow for inheritance, meaning that programmers can build on what is already contained in the object without having to start from scratch. Gardner explains how he works with languages that are object oriented:

> In object-oriented languages, like C++ and Java, I am working with objects [that I pull together to create a program]. Each object encapsulates [contains] a piece of logic—an instruction to the computer on how to process a piece of work. Objects allow me to complete a task without being concerned with the steps the computer must take to get there. [For example] I can use an object to tell

Programmer Integrity

In The Philosophical Programmer, Reflections on the Moth in the Machine, *Daniel Kohanski discusses the importance of ethics for computer programmers. He makes the interesting point that once programmers complete their work, the computer must do what it is supposed to do without further oversight by the programmer. He believes this "autonomy of operation" is one reason why programmers must approach their work with a great deal of integrity:*

From a programmer's perspective, the ethical implication of this autonomy of operation is that it demands a meticulous attention to detail. The programmer is preparing a series of instructions to be given to a computer to execute while the programmer is no longer there. And the computer has no leeway or latitude in carrying out its orders except those the programmer has given it; thus each instruction must be precise and clear, and in some way deal with all the possibilities that the program can confront. The programmer's responsibility is far more consuming that that of an officer giving a command to a troop of soldiers, who are expected to use judgment and good sense in carrying out their orders. The computer has neither.

the computer to get certain information from a database. The steps it takes are contained in the object, meaning I don't have to be concerned with those steps myself.[11]

Finding and Correcting Bugs

Once a program has been written, programmers evaluate it to make sure it works as it should and that users will find it appealing. Programmers use special software that looks for errors—commonly referred to as bugs. When errors are found, programmers correct them. This process is called debugging a program. Bugs can have several causes. For instance, programmers may input instructions in an order that interferes with how the program looks on the computer screen. Gardner explains how the tiniest misstep can wreak havoc: "Just a single period, comma, or quotation mark out of place can throw off thousands of lines of perfect work. Also, because of the complex nature of some programming, an application can be run a million times without error, then be run one extra time with just the right combination of factors that cause it to crash [freeze or stop working]."[12]

Philadelphia International Airport appears deserted on January 1, 2000. Many travelers feared Y2K computer problems would cripple air-travel systems.

After the initial debugging, companies test their programs by putting them to use. The first stage of testing, which occurs within the company developing the software, is called alpha testing. The next phase is beta testing, during which users outside the company (such as prospective customers) are invited to try the new program either at home or at a beta testing center. After any needed adjustments are made, gamma, the final testing phase, takes place just before the new product is marketed.

Programmers are aided in the evaluation process by coworkers who specialize in quality assurance. The point of quality assurance is to have someone who can step back from the programmer's product and handle it the way users in the real world will: unpredictably. While programmers may feel confident about the work they have done, they must be open to the possibility that users will have different experiences and, of course, the programmer must be ready to make changes. *Liberty*, who wrote *The Complete Idiot's Guide to a Career in Computer Programming*, describes one of his early experiences with a quality assurance professional who tested Liberty's new software program by trying things that most programmers would never think of but that users might do for reasons that computer "geeks" would neither understand nor anticipate.

> Some years ago, I was working on software for an online service when the director of QA [quality assurance] called me and told me that a module [a part of a program] I'd submitted for review was crashing. "Impossible," I said with great confidence. "I tested it fully." She walked to my desk and said, "Fire it up." I did. "Click here." I did that, too. "Now enter 5 here." Before I could stop myself, I blurted out, "No one would do that!" She just walked away chuckling.[13]

Programming for the Real World

Anticipating how users will react to a program is an important part of good programming. Some programmers, like Jen McGrath who works for the search engine Google, become experts in user interface, the process of making sure that programs can be easily used by, and are appealing to, software customers. She explains

Communicating with the Computer

In Data Structures and Algorithms in C++, *the authors, Michael T. Goodrich, Roberto Tamassia, and David M. Mount, explain that high-level languages are useful tools to instruct computers to perform the demanding tasks that Americans take for granted at the dawn of the twenty-first century. The authors use the technical language: "data structure," which they define as "a systematic way of organizing and accessing data," and "algorithm," which they define as "a step-by-step procedure for performing some task in a finite amount of time."*

Modern computers routinely have memory capacities that are tens of millions of times larger than ENIAC [the first digital computer, built in 1945] ever had, and memory capacities continue to grow at astonishing rates. This growth in capacity has brought with it a new and exciting role for computers. Rather than simply being fast calculators, modern computers are *information processors*. They store, analyze, search, transfer, and update huge collections of complex data. Quickly performing these tasks requires that data be well organized and that the methods for accessing and maintaining data be fast and efficient. In short, modern computers need good data structures and algorithms. Specifying these data structures and algorithms requires that we communicate instructions to a computer, and an excellent way to perform such communication is using a high-level computer language, such as C++.

her work in this area: "User interface design work . . . involves thinking about the look and feel of any new products or features that we release on our site, both in terms of their design and in terms of . . . user interaction."[14] Thus, user interface experts consider such things as whether word processing toolbars—symbols that appear at the top or side of the screen to allow users to do things such as adding footnotes and moving text—can be easily understood and worked by the user.

Like much of the work done by programmers, user interface has an intuitive side to it. While it might be hard to put into words why a program is appealing (or not), some programmers have a better feel for it than others. One commentator, Daniel Kohanski, calls this intangible quality of programming skill the aesthetic of programming. He explains that an essential part of making these good decisions is considering the impact of one's programming instructions in the long run. In other words, even though something fixes, or works for, a problem today, it may cause problems in the future or, in the alternative, may not allow for evolutionary changes without a great deal of hassle. Kohanski cites as an example one of the most famous instances of a lack of aesthetic sensitivity—the early programming that resulted in the "Y2K" crisis at the end of the twentieth century. This crisis required a staggering effort to reprogram computers so that all of the societal functions that rely on proper dating, from collecting loan payments to issuing social security checks to running machines and computers, would not be disrupted:

> A dramatic example of this insufficient attention to consequences is the potential for disaster presented by the year 2000 problem. Early computers, and the punched cards they used for input, were very short on space and often used a two-digit field to represent the year, Everyone understood that "50" meant "1950." But no one stopped to think that a computer program that interpreted "50" as "1950" would also interpret "00" as "1900" instead of 2000—or if some did think about it, they thought that a program written in 1950 would be long gone by the turn of the century.[15]

Near Perfection Required

Of course, in addition to having a good sense of the future impact of one's work, programmers have excellent technical skills, are hyper detail oriented, and enjoy doing and redoing a project to get it just right. Persistence and perfectionism are two essential qualities for programmers because so much of the success of their work is based on miniscule details, which, if wrong, must be hunted down and corrected by the programmer. Creating error-free programs is not simply a matter of satisfaction for programmers and their employers. In certain cases, such as this described by expert programmer and author Schildt, doing an excellent job may be a matter of life and death:

> In large programs, especially those that control potentially life-threatening events, the potential for error has to be very slight. Although small programs can be verified as correct, this is not the case for large ones. (A verified program is proved to be free of errors and will never malfunction—in theory at least.) For example, consider a program that controls the wing flaps of a modern jet airplane. You cannot test all possible interactions of the numerous forces that will be exerted on the plane. This means that you cannot test the program exhaustively. At best, all that you can say is that it performed correctly in such and such situations. In a program of this type, the last thing that you (as a passenger or programmer) want is a crash (of the program or the plane).[16]

While they are careful to complete all of their work consistently with acceptable procedures, programmers are also innovators, people willing to try something new to address a problem they may be the first to define or understand. One forward-thinking programmer is Dimitri Kanevsky, who developed a program that allows computers to recognize human voices. A cell phone's understanding of a verbal command to dial a number and a computer's ability to transcribe a user's speech are two functions in common use today in which Kanevsky played a significant part. He credits his creative approach to solving voice-recognition software problems to the fact that he is deaf. "I considered speech more mathematically and tried to find mathematical patterns rather than acoustic ones,"[17] he told journalist David Robinson.

Dedication to Perfection

While many computer technology workplaces became more formal as companies grew from new entities to more established ones at the end of the twentieth century, programmers are still part of a culture that grew out of informal work atmospheres. Laid-back workplaces—where employees show up in shorts and running shoes and work the schedules that suit them—can still be found. However, going to work dressed casually is not the same

A man wearing a suit works with an early computer in 1946. Today, programmers work in informal environments, often wearing shorts and running shoes to work.

thing as taking one's work lightly. Computer programmers are part of a breed of workers who are highly dedicated, as illustrated by author William A. Schaffer: "[High tech is] the only industry I know of where folks working on a deadline take sleeping bags to work and curl up under their desks for forty winks, before getting back to business at two or three in the morning."[18]

One way to avoid sleepovers at work is to work at home. Telecommuting is becoming more common because it saves wear and tear on workers and gives them flexibility during the work-week. However, while working at home seems like an advantage for parents or others who cannot be away from home for long

Tackling New Problems

Max Gardner is a recent college graduate who, in 2003, began working as a software developer with a New York telecommunications company. In an e-mail interview with the author, Gardner explains how he started in the career, and gives helpful advice to those interested in becoming programmers:

I began programming when I was thirteen because I found it interesting. Then I applied for—and got—an internship at Qualcomm [the San Diego–based company that pioneered wireless technologies for cell phones and many other functions]. Everything seemed to take off from there. The experience, skills, and relationships you get from each job help you get the next one. Just keep your eyes open and take advantage of opportunities as they arise. Don't be afraid to push yourself to tackle problems you're not 100 percent sure you can handle, or else you'll never grow professionally.

hours at a time, having one's office available twenty-four hours a day can create another kind of stress: It is often hard to avoid stopping in to work at the home office, even after business hours.

Because programming requires many, many hours of time at the computer, besides feeling overworked, programmers may experience physical problems, such as carpal tunnel syndrome (wrist pain that may require surgery), eye strain, and aching backs. In addition, for some workers, the constant challenge associated with developing and perfecting programs can be difficult. People who are not perfectionists, have a low tolerance for frustration, or tend to personalize criticism may not be happy in programming.

Self-Teaching and Coursework

Programmers solve problems, and perhaps the best way to train for this career is to venture into programming by learning on one's own. Finding that one enjoys this exploration and the process of trying, failing, then trying and succeeding, will help a future programmer determine if the field is right for them.

Learning on one's own does not mean figuring things out in a vacuum. In fact, programmers recommend using the Internet to uncover the work other programmers have done and to read manuals that guide the process. Gardner explains some of the factors that helped him as he got up to speed in programming:

> The most helpful thing I did was choose projects that excited and motivated me. If you're not interested in the overall project, it's hard to force yourself to learn something difficult and new. The great thing about programming is that there's so much free example code available on the Internet. It's likely that anything you want to do has been done before by someone else. The best way to learn is by watching others and asking questions.[19]

In addition to developing experience on one's own, those in computer fields may get undergraduate degrees. While in 2000 only three-fifths of programmers had bachelor's or graduate degrees, having at least a bachelor's degree is expected to become the norm in the twenty-first century. Applicable undergraduate degrees vary from those in computer or information science to mathematics, engineering, and business. This is most likely because programmers are the types of people who learn the nitty-gritty aspects of their crafts on their own and benefit, therefore, as much from a general education as from a more specific one.

Instead of or in addition to college coursework, programmers may become certified by taking courses and passing exams. These courses are sponsored by companies that make hardware and software (for example, Microsoft) or by associations that specialize in the computer field. These certifications are meant to show that a person has a very narrow type of expertise, and they require the programmer to study the ins and outs of programming in specific languages. As online writer Andrew Carter explains: "There's no catch-all . . . certification. Rather, certifications are specific to certain technologies and job descriptions."[20]

Experts caution that in today's competitive market, while certification may help if it is one part of a professional's overall experience, employers do not view certification as a substitute for time on a job. Also, while some students see a benefit because they can earn a certificate much faster than an undergraduate degree and

While many programmers prefer the challenge of teaching themselves, many others take classes to improve their skills.

thus enter the workplace sooner, companies most often look for employees with a well-rounded education, which is shown by an undergraduate degree.

Long Hours Pay Off

Although they may not have had a set path for entering their careers, median earnings in 2000 for programmers with or without degrees were almost $60,000, with some individuals making as little as $35,000 and others over $93,210. However, salary studies show that because there was less demand, programmers lost a few percentage points in wages between 2000 and 2003.

Many people in this profession experienced disheartening layoffs at the turn of the century. However, jobs for programmers are expected to grow about as fast as the average for all other jobs through 2010, according to the Bureau of Labor Statistics, which attributes this less-than-spectacular growth to the fact that software has become more sophisticated, eliminating the need for programmers to complete certain tasks.

Even though jobs will be harder to get, programming is a highly satisfying field for those who have a passion for writing code. Gardner expresses the enthusiasm common among programmers this way:

The great thing about software development is that it's totally dynamic. I'm always learning. New languages and technologies are constantly emerging, which means my job never gets stale. Programming is also a very creative process. It's all about finding the most elegant and powerful solution to a given problem, and there are always many different ways to accomplish the same end result. Finding the best way that balances speed, power, and other requirements is very challenging, but fun.[21]

Chapter 2

Network Administrators

Network administrators oversee computer networks. They work to facilitate, maintain, and troubleshoot the vital communication links between computers within a company and between company computers and the Internet. They oversee the equipment and applications that make this network of computers run smoothly, including hardware, software, operating systems, and servers, as well as routers and switches that control information and data flow and traffic. Without network administrators, most companies could not function in the technological world of the twenty-first century. Administrators manage many different critical links in a network of computers that connects a company's employees to each other and to valuable resources outside of the company, allowing networks to function efficiently and without interruption. They also take steps to protect the network from malicious attacks from viruses and from technological failures and glitches that can lead to a loss of data or an interruption of work.

Network administrators work in any type of business that has a network of computers. This includes banks, hospitals, universities, governmental agencies, and manufacturers.

Overseeing the LAN and WAN

Networks are typically called either local area networks (LANs)—computers connected within one building—or wide area networks (WANs)—computers connected from one building to another. Company computers are also connected to the Internet. Network administrators are charged with keeping all of these functions working, which includes preventing damage from viruses that may enter a company's networks from the Internet.

26

In *Cisco Networking Simplified*, authors Paul Della Maggiora and Jim Doherty summarize the importance of the administrator:

> A network administrator is responsible for the health and well-being of a company's network. Her goal generally is to provide uninterrupted network services. If a network outage or fault occurs, she wants to know about it as soon as possible and isolate the problem quickly . . . to restore business operations. . . . [When the network is not working] a manufacturing line might stop operating. Or a stock-trading firm might stop trading. A hospital might lose the ability to track patients. A theme park might be unable to collect tickets.[22]

Monitoring the system is an important daily function of administrators. This may be as simple as looking at equipment

Network administrators maintain computer networks that may consist of computers housed in one building or in several different buildings or locations.

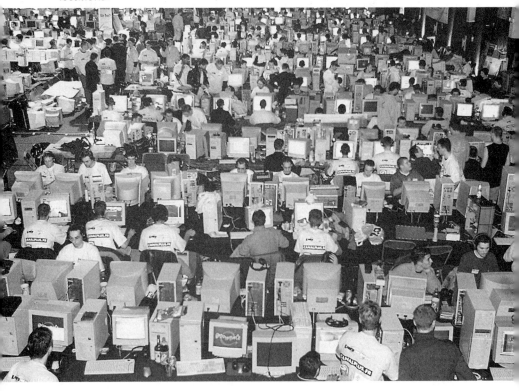

and making sure there are no obvious physical problems, such as wires that are frayed or plugged into the wrong connection. More and more often, administrators use technology itself as a tool to monitor the health of the unseen parts of the network. For instance, they may install on the network software that tracks the amount of electricity being used by the system. A product review describes how administrators use such tools: "Network administrators can monitor how much current is being used and avoid circuit-breaker trips that would shut down a system."[23] If administrators learn that the network is using too much electricity, they take preventive steps (temporarily reducing the number of computers in use) then work to upgrade the network to better accommodate the company's desired use.

Systems Analyst

Systems analyst is another career for those interested in helping businesses meet their technological needs. While administrators are concerned with the physical workings of computer networks, the systems analyst acts as a consultant to help businesses improve all aspects of the flow of information in a business. As an example, an analyst who works for a new online shoe company may be asked to set up a system that will allow the company to take, fill, and keep track of new orders. Because such a system impacts many different departments in the company—from marketing to buying (at the wholesale level) to shipping—the analyst interviews managers in the different areas to get a sense of how the process should work. The analyst makes many different types of analyses, including those that determine the relative costs of different hardware and software solutions, then prepares a report making recommendations to upper managers. The analyst implements the system decided on, a complex task that involves writing specifications and drawing flowcharts that will help programmers code the new system. Systems analysts oftentimes have bachelor's or master's degrees in computer-science-related fields such as information systems. They earned an average of about sixty thousand dollars a year in 2000.

Administrators may also be called on to help companies monitor not just the equipment but also the users, the company employees. For instance, administrators install network software that tracks how employees use their computers. Administrators review the data produced by these types of programs and respond to protect the interests of the company. For instance, they may advise management if they learn that a certain employee is playing games online instead of working.

One way that administrators manage networks is to document how the network is connected—in other words, how the various devices in the network link up. Administrators create diagrams and charts to show this and to map the many cables that run from one office to another. They create databases that show which users are using which Internet protocol addresses so that they can go directly to the location of a problem. Della Maggiora explains how the process of documentation can smooth teamwork: "Where more than a couple of people are responsible for a network, you need change-control documentation. Change control is the process of documenting any changes to the network *before* you make them so a group can review the changes and ensure that one set of changes doesn't overwrite another."[24]

Updating the network with new hardware or software is another way that administrators ensure trouble-free functioning of LANs and WANs. To accomplish this, they keep up with new technologies as well as updates and improvements from manufacturers of software and hardware currently in use by the administrator's company. They also keep in touch with their company's networking goals by attending meetings. When changes are decided on, how to implement them with the least possible disruption to network users can be the subject of intense debate among administrators and others, such as department managers, with an interest in keeping work flowing. Administrators test changes in a limited part of the network or on a dummy system and keep track of what they have done for future reference. They may work outside of normal office hours to implement the change, thus causing as little disruption as possible.

Specializing

Because so much expertise is needed in these fields, people tend to specialize. For instance, they may become experts in an individual operating system such as Linux or Windows NT, or highly skilled troubleshooters, or, they may become involved in hands-on work, such as building servers and installing hardware. Finding a path that will remain valuable to employers, even as the company's needs change and new operating systems come and go, is key to continued success in administration. Authors Drew Bird and Mike Harwood address this situation in *Information Technology Careers: The Hottest Jobs for the New Millennium:* "The solution, if you are interested in specialization, is to become specialized in a technology rather than a product. Technologies tend to evolve, whereas products are often replaced."[25]

Vincent Mase, an expert at data recovery, says that, like many in his field, he fell into his specialty. He is available to recover lost data in a crisis, but his real job is to make sure that this extreme point is reached as rarely as possible. Mase explains the different steps involved in this important aspect of his job:

> The first tier [of defense against losing data] is to build fault tolerance into the system. This includes making sure that the server has alternate cards and multiple hard drives so that a hot spare can take over [if the main hard drive fails]. The second tier is to make sure that data is backed up in case there is malicious destruction through a virus or some other kind of attack. The third tier is to plan for recovery. This means that software and hardware are replicated at another place, so if a company building in Boston blows up or burns down an alternate location in, say, San Diego could take over within five seconds.[26]

Network security is a specialty that is becoming more and more important in the twenty-first century, because businesses are increasingly experiencing threats to their networks. In fact, one report estimates that over eighty thousand security problems occurred in American businesses in the first half of 2003. Security breaches can occur from the outside, as with worms (programs sent to unsuspecting computer users over the Internet that can seriously interfere with computer functioning) such as Sobig.F, or from the inside. For instance, a disgruntled employee may try to steal customer data that can include sensitive information, such as credit card and social security numbers. While employees can

Hackers test new security programs during a computer security conference. Demand is soaring for professionals who specialize in computer security.

wreak havoc, viruses from the Internet are a nightmare for network administrators and their clients because they can rapidly infect computers in an entire system, causing a loss of valuable data or the crashing of workstations. As journalist Lou Dolinar wrote about the worm Sobig.F: "Anything was possible, from denial of service attacks against major Web sites to harvesting of address books for commercial spammers."[27]

The goal for administrators is to keep attackers from breaking into the system in the first place (for instance, by linking a virus to an e-mail attachment) and to make sure that if they do break in, they do not have access to all the data in the system. Administrators accomplish this by building up protection between different sections of data on the server. As one method of keeping out unwanted intruders, administrators install firewalls—on personal computers (PCs) themselves and at the perimeter where ports (pathways into and out of the network) can allow entry into the system. Firewalls can be added to hardware or to software and can take one of a number of different formats (or a combination), which include filtering or intercepting incoming and outgoing data based on rules (such as having recognizable Internet addresses) that administrators define.

A Delicate Balance

Installing a software manufacturer's repair patches (program adjustments that make computers less vulnerable to attack) on individual computers is also a way of rebutting attacks, but it is a task that can be daunting in large companies that have hundreds or thousands of desktop computers in one or more locations. Thus, dealing with security issues is just one area where administrators are called upon to walk a delicate balance between what they think is best, the opinions and budgets of their employers, and the current workings of the system. For instance, one commentator, Alex Salkever, suggests that administrators may hesitate to use security patches because they know that changing the balance of software programs can create major problems: "[Patches can] interfere with other software running on the machine. No one wants to

Computer Forensics

Network security is an important function of network administrators. Computer forensics is a related field. It addresses crimes that are committed or can be solved with computers. This field is expected to grow dramatically in the twenty-first century in response to a growing number of computer-related crimes. Computer-forensics professionals use a number of sophisticated methods to track down those people responsible for sending computer viruses, to uncover evidence that is useful in criminal or civil court cases, and to fight crime and terrorism. Professionals in this field are typically law enforcement officers who receive training in computer science, or computer professionals who receive training in law enforcement. They work in security firms, corporations, and law enforcement and other government agencies. They often testify in court about their findings and methods.

explain to the senior vice-president of marketing that his or her personal-contacts database crashed because of a patch."[28]

Productivity is key in all companies, and this means that administrators must be careful not to make any changes that will unduly interfere with work. Marc Spiwak, in reviewing a new product to help make security products more efficient, discusses the problem with many existing technologies: "Standard security solutions tend to slow things down. Network administrators must therefore compromise between keeping networks secure and allowing reasonable access to them."[29]

Even beyond issues of security, making sure that the system does not get out of whack is a fundamental job of administrators. It is especially important when administrators add new hardware and software, because they must be careful not to create one problem when trying to solve another. For instance, new programs exist that allow for the automatic updating of firmware (software that is integral to hardware produced by the same company). These programs could be useful because administrators spend a great deal of the time doing updates manually. However, as with every other step administrators take, providing for automatic updates can have unintended consequences. In discussing a new product that self-updates firmware (without the individual efforts of administrators), reviewer David Strom wrote of his experience: "When you start making changes to a smoothly running network, the more that changes the more difficult it is for an administrator to troubleshoot and fix something that breaks."[30] To avoid problems, Strom suggests that administrators be vigilant about documenting and mapping their networks so they can trace any negative changes caused by the automatic update.

Anonymity and Independence

The complexities of the network make the administrator's job challenging for several reasons. If networks crash, the administrator may experience a significant amount of pressure from coworkers to get things working again. In these circumstances, administrators may have to put in long hours, sometimes in the evening or on weekends. Even in the normal course of business, dealing with coworkers and supervisors can be difficult. This is because it is often hard to explain to laypersons why solutions are not available to every problem. Thus, the expectation that administrators can make magic is one of the most challenging aspects of these jobs. And when they do accomplish extraordinary things, they often suffer from a lack of recognition. As Mase sees it: "I'm like the goalie. No one notices me until something goes wrong. I could roll out a great data recovery system, but unless someone is looking for data that I can't recover, nobody really seems to care what I do."[31]

Both of these negatives—a lack of recognition and the pressure that comes from running a network that is vital to a company's functioning—have positive flip sides. Network administrators have a satisfying amount of autonomy in their work. Mase describes this aspect of his experience: "As long as you keep up your skills, you can pretty much do what you want. No one is looking over your shoulder, because, in fact, no one understands whether you are doing your job well or not. I'm so busy doing things nobody ever sees that no one knows if I'm doing my job or not."[32]

In addition, administration requires the constant updating of skills and a response to situations that vary from day to day. Thus, administrators find that their work remains stimulating, even after they have been doing it for a number of years.

Income and Advancement Opportunities

According to online career company WetFeet, network administrators earn between $45,000 and $75,000 a year. Administrators earn the higher salaries after they have gained experience. In addition, those who work for large companies with extensive LANs or WANs tend to earn more. Certification can also help increase pay. According to the Institute for Certification of Computing Professionals (ICCP), obtaining certification through their organization can lead to annual increases of $6,000 to $18,000, while earning a certificate from a specific computer company such as Microsoft will result in a smaller increase, in the $4,000 to $5,000 range.

Network administrators can increase their income by advancing to administer larger networks or by becoming managers who oversee the activities of more junior network administrators. Administrators with college degrees, especially those with a master of business administration, can advance to become information systems directors or managers. These higher-level employees oversee the technological needs of a company and participate in budgeting, planning, and hiring. They can earn salaries in the $80,000 range for managers and over $100,000 for directors.

A Varied Approach to Education

Network administrators do not have a clearly defined educational path, but about 60 percent have a bachelor's degree in some subject, although often not in a technical area. Technical degrees that would be helpful include those in electronics, computer science, and information technology. Administrators learn mostly on the job, although some take certification courses given by manufacturers of the various systems they administer or take more general training in community colleges.

Becoming certified requires passing one or more tests in a narrow area of study. Certification may be through programs sponsored by computer companies (vendor certification) such as Microsoft. Another company, Cisco, runs the Cisco Network Academy Program, which offers training for its own and other companies' products on-line and in many different locations, including regional occupational programs given at high schools. Certification is also offered by professional associations such as the ICCP. Certification is granted at different levels, depending on how advanced a student is. Courses vary depending on the focus of the certification program. They include topics such as the basics of networking and troubleshooting, the best ways

Network administrators who work for large companies like Compaq which is now part of Hewlett-Packard company often earn higher salaries.

to maintain a network and make it safe, and how to run specific operating systems, such as Microsoft Windows NT.

Certification exams are challenging, but as the ICCP website explains, even those who do not pass the first time benefit: "A significant number of people fail the ICCP examination. But all examination takers receive a detailed breakdown of their skills, strengths and weaknesses (gap analysis), which they then use as a guide to plan their professional development program."[33]

Technical schools, community colleges, and some universities offer training specific to administrators, including coursework that leads to specialization in computer and network security. In one innovative program in England, student network administrators are working with computer simulations of a host of networking problems that are faced on a regular basis. These classes take place at Leeds Metropolitan University, where Colin Pattinson has devised for his undergraduate and graduate students a chance

Certification

The *Occupational Outlook Quarterly* reported in a Fall 2002 article "Training for Techies: Career Preparation in Information Technology," that over one hundred vendors offer nearly seven hundred different certificate programs. However, although such programs are widespread, employers debate the value of them, with some preferring that prospective employees instead complete community college or university degrees or gain on-the-job experience. However, the article's author, Roger Moncarz, predicts that certification will continue to be a valued way to show that an employee has a specific skill, such as in network security. In addition, sponsors of certification programs point to their value in helping young people start computer technology careers and seasoned workers make career changes, because the certifications can be completed by taking a series of courses on-line or in the evening. This process can be completed more quickly and with a level of flexibility that is helpful for those with other commitments such as families or full-time jobs in other fields.

to experience an increasingly complex series of network failures and keep track of the solutions they devise. Pattinson explains: "Dedicated screens show the build-up and causes of a fault situation and show what distress signals the system will send out to enable an early diagnosis."[34]

A Promising Future

New teaching techniques, such as the example above, may be helpful because, even with all the innovations of the twentieth century behind them, administrators will be required to learn new things. For instance, while much of the administrator's work once centered on keeping servers functional and up to date, Mase sees a different path for them in the twenty-first century: "The server is becoming an almost nonexistent thing. Instead, companies will have one big powerful computer that will present as twenty computers, and can host any operating system. It will have the ability to look like as many servers as it needs to."[35]

In addition, administrators will benefit from continually updating their skills in computer security, an area that the Bureau of Labor Statistics characterizes as an emerging specialty. Olivia Crosby explains in *Occupational Outlook Quarterly:* "In most companies, the same workers who set up and administer computer networks also keep them secure. But as security tasks become more numerous and complex, computer workers have begun to specialize, even earning specific credentials and degrees."[36] The chance to develop new and challenging specialties makes a career as network administrator appealing to many. In addition, career experts recommend network administration because these workers are expected to be in very high demand in the first decade of the twenty-first century.

Chapter 3

Hardware Engineers

Hardware engineers are experts in computer hardware. They think up, develop, and create new computer hardware technologies and update old ones. Hardware engineers are primarily concerned with the physical parts of the computer and all the peripherals that work with it. Hardware refers not only to the physical parts of the computer that can be seen from the outside, but also to the most important parts that are hidden inside the case. In *The whatis?com Encyclopedia of Technology Terms*, the evolution of the term *hardware* is explained this way:

> The term arose as a way to distinguish the "box" and the electronic circuitry and components of a computer from the program you put in it to make it do things. . . . Hardware is a collective term. Hardware includes not only the computer proper but also the cables, connectors, power supply units, and peripheral devices, such as the keyboard, mouse, audio speakers, and printers.[37]

Hardware engineers work in many different settings. These include hardware and telecommunications companies, university and government research labs, and companies that make electronics and semiconductors.

Brainstorming and Designing

Engineers begin the hardware development process by brainstorming. This important activity takes place in meetings with other engineers and those in the company guiding the project. The purpose of these meetings is to define the overall goals of a project and outline the best way to achieve those goals. Author

Julie Kling Burns summarizes the activities of computer engineers at this early stage: "A hardware product begins as an idea or a concept. A team of engineers and computer science experts get together and ask: 'What would we (or our customers) like to see in a product? What problem can we solve?'"[38]

After these initial discussions, engineers begin the long process of planning and drafting specifications for the project. The exact nature of these specifications depends on what is being designed. For instance, the hardware engineer may be designing the more visible parts of the hardware, such as the computer case

Steve Wozniak, cofounder of Apple Computer, is a hardware engineer. Hardware engineers work with the physical components of a computer.

or a mouse, or one of the internal components that make it possible for the computer to think, such as the central processing unit (CPU), the central brain of the computer.

Hardware engineers decide on the design of the CPU and each of the other electrical components. This involves not only deciding on the size and shape of a part, but also where each part will be placed in relation to other parts. This is an exacting task, because it involves figuring out how electricity will flow between the components.

The design phase may take weeks, months, or years and requires engineers to use software that helps create models and drawings of the new equipment. An article by Roger Moncarz in the *Occupational Outlook Quarterly* explains that engineers use CAD (computer aided design programs) "to create digital models of objects that can then be manipulated by computer. They might also use CAD to create complete prototypes of designs."[39] In some cases, engineers oversee the work of CAD technicians instead of doing CAD design themselves. Engineers rely on extensive feedback from other engineers and company personnel, including those in marketing and manufacturing, to determine if the design will work best for the intended purpose.

New but Not Always Useful

Hardware engineers are increasingly experimenting with technology in the twenty-first century. For instance, engineers have created devices that allow users to take their computers with them. These include invisible screens made up of water particles on which data and images can be projected and wearable computers with monitors the size of eye patches that display cursors manipulated by the user's thumb. However individuals testing these technologies are not always convinced of their convenience or usefulness. Some experts believe that, even as the physical design of personal computers evolves to match new trends in material or color and to accommodate improved portability, the original concept will remain: a machine that includes a monitor, a processor, and a keyboard.

Engineers supervise the manufacturing department as they build prototypes based on the design. The design may be for a large hardware component or for a smaller piece. For example, Pete Jarvis works on hardware logic, which is made up of circuits that perform important operations. Getting the wiring in the right place is essential to making the computer work initially and then with maximum efficiency. He explains the process of reviewing his design this way: "My day begins with looking at . . . [the results of system tests] and determining whether or not we need to make changes in the design or changes in the process to achieve better results."[40] This process of debugging is extremely important and may lead to critical adjustments that must be made before a product is ready to go to manufacturing and then, ultimately, be sold to businesses or consumers. Because of the many steps involved, the process of developing and manufacturing new equipment takes months or years.

Precision Required

Designing hardware takes a certain amount of vision. Thus, engineers must be savvy not only about the nuts and bolts of design and manufacturing, but they must also consider the implications of the design choices they make. These factors include how to achieve good user interface (sometimes with the help of those who specialize in this), how efficiently the product will operate, and the cost to manufacture the item. Small details can have a big impact on this last factor, and engineers consider them, sometimes with the help of others in the company, such as people who specialize in shipping or who oversee the manufacturing end and understand what goes on at the assembly line and what can save time and costs there. Engineers use special software to visualize what the building of their designs will entail. For instance, one software program, called Design for Assembly, helped a team of engineers eliminate some of the screws previously used to make a desktop computer. Each screw eliminated cut eight seconds off the production time of each computer, thus significantly reducing costs.

Teamwork

One way engineers work to further the business goals of their employers is to act as liaisons with their customers, gaining feedback about existing products and getting ideas for new ones.

During visits to the offices of their customers, engineers may make presentations about products and answer questions. In these instances, as within their own company, engineers are often called upon to communicate technical ideas and recommendations to those who are not technical experts: for instance, to bosses who make decisions about how to proceed based not just on the issues that interest the engineer, but also after giving due consideration to budgeting and policy.

Engineers may work as part of small groups or huge teams that require a massive amount of coordination. In this instance, engineers also turn to technology to help them accomplish goals, using special management software to keep track of the project and team members. In "Project-Coordination Tools: Get Your Act Together Before You Take It on the Road," Bill Schweber describes how large and complex some engineering projects can become:

> The software tracks instructions to team members, personnel reassignments, team resources, work assignments, and team relationships. It also recognizes the unavoidable fact that team members may leave the company. It associates instructions with both the name of the team member and the member's role, so roles can be reassigned as necessary.[41]

Diverse Skills and Corporate Challenges

While technical skills are essential, because so much of their job involves teamwork and interaction with management and customers, engineers must be good communicators and good team players. For this reason, Jeff Baer, software manager, has this advice for aspiring engineers: "Take a presentation class. It's miserable, but even engineers have to do presentations and if you're good at it, it's easier and you'll go a lot further in your career."[42]

Engineers are highly intelligent, logical thinkers, and have excellent abstract spatial abilities and dexterity so they can visualize and build projects. They are excellent mathematicians and persistent perfectionists. Also much of their work involves juggling deadlines and projects effectively in order to meet deadlines. These are skills the engineer must have or develop.

Because hardware engineers often work in teams, they must be good communicators and team players.

Because of these demands, hardware engineers may experience high levels of stress. They may also have to work long hours to complete projects on time and to keep up with the latest trends in their industry. In addition, engineers, like others in corporate America, may have to contend with office politics and, as with other highly technical fields, coworkers with big egos.

Many Options for Degrees

Hardware engineers typically have at least a bachelor's degree, and electrical engineering is a traditional major. However, increasingly in the twenty-first century, these professionals will become multidisciplinary, gaining additional training and education in fields such as mechanical engineering, biology, and telecommunications. Thus many different majors are valuable for those who aspire to become hardware engineers. These include physics, materials science, electrical systems design, robotics, automated systems, and engineering technology. Many universities are combining majors in innovative ways. For instance, undergraduate students at the University of California San Diego who enroll in the Department of Computer Science and Engineering can obtain bachelor of science degrees in computer science and computer engineering, or a bachelor of arts degree in computer science, which allows for more courses outside of computer science and engineering.

Undergraduate students in the Department of Computer Science and Engineering take courses in mathematics, physics, and electrical engineering. Electrical engineering study includes laboratory classes in which students study semiconductor devices and digital electronics. In a circuits and systems laboratory, stu-

Women in Science, Engineering, and Technology

In September 2000, the Congressional Commission on the Advancement of Women and Minorities in Science, Engineering and Technology Development issued a report called "Land of Plenty, Diversity as America's Competitive Edge in Science, Engineering and Technology." The report documents how these groups are underrepresented in science, engineering, and technology (SET) careers and suggests ways to close the gap, including improved education and enrichment and role modeling. The report also points out that while girls are getting good scientific and mathematical educations, societal expectations still influence their career choices:

Even while girls' achievement in SET increases, their interest and participation in science and mathematics continues to go down. A combination of factors likely accounts for this paradox. Girls' rejection of mathematics and science interests may be partially driven by teachers, parents, and peers when they subtly, and not so subtly, steer girls away from the kind of informal technical pastimes (working on cars, fixing bicycles, changing hardware on the computer) and science activities (science fairs, science clubs) that too often are still thought of as the province of boys. Data show that girls are indeed less likely than boys to be involved in informal science and mathematics activities outside of school, from using meters and playing with electromagnets to fixing machines and reading about technology. Additionally, media and real-life images of women in scientific and technical careers are still rare (as are female role models and mentors, in general), sending an unspoken message to girls that a SET career is not for them.

dents can make models and design circuits. Experienced engineers suggest that students find ways of getting experience building hardware, even if it is not offered as part of the school experience. In addition, learning Verilog, a language used to design electronic systems, is recommended.

Universities also offer master's and PhD degrees. Engineers interested in doing advanced research and teaching will go on to obtain a PhD. Obtaining the degree takes several years beyond the undergraduate degree and requires the student to complete original research and pass difficult, comprehensive, oral and written examinations.

Salaries Reflect Supply and Demand

Successful engineers develop the expertise needed to do their jobs and their salaries reflect this factor. According to the Bureau of Labor Statistics, hardware engineers earned a median annual salary of $67,300 in 2000, with the range from lowest to highest being $42,620 to over $100,000. Engineers with master's degrees made about 10 percent more than those with bachelor's degrees. Those with a PhD average in the $70,000 range. However, salary studies reported by CNNmoney online in 2003 showed that hardware engineers lost ground, in fact, up to 7.6 percent of their salaries, because there were more hardware engineers looking for work than companies looking to hire them.

Engineers may advance or find other opportunities by becoming senior engineers or managers who oversee the hardware products for their companies. If they earn a PhD, they can become university professors or computer scientists, and thus become involved in the highest levels of research and development of new computer technologies.

Emerging Technologies

Hardware engineers of the twenty-first century will continue to try to improve on the basic PC by finding ways to make computers more and more portable through wireless and other technologies that free users from their desks. At the dawn of the twenty-first century, computer companies gave birth to tablets, which are electronic "writing" pads that read the user's handwriting and send the data to a computer. New technologies evolve in response to the needs of many different types of consumers—from home computer users to businesses and hospitals. For instance, telemedicine is a way for doctors to communicate with other doctors far away, allowing a well-known clinic, such as the Mayo Clinic in Rochester, Minnesota, to help a rural doctor who does not have access to the same research and expert staff. In San Diego, California, engineers are working to dramatically improve the processing speed of computers by using fiber optics for connections between computer components. According to journalist Patricia Daukantas, San Diego Supercomputer Center program director Philip M. Papadopoulos believes this development, called high-bandwith computing, "could make telemedicine easier by speeding the transfer of large data files from medical imaging devices."[43]

Engineers of the twenty-first century will become involved in a host of new fields of study that even a few years earlier were not imagined, let alone part of the popular culture of ideas. Many new fields are interdisciplinary in nature, meaning that computer engineers and researchers will increasingly work with other professionals or be expected to cross train to achieve new and better technologies. For instance, "mechatronics" merges sophisticated software, with mechanics to improve how machines, such as cars,

A college student works in a computer science lab. Hardware engineers with a higher education often make higher salaries.

Taking a Risk?

In Careers Inside the Computer Industry, *Julie Kling Burns outlines the potential upside and downside of going to work for a start-up, a new company that is developing an innovative product:*

The rewards for working at a successful start-up can be enormous. Many of the wealthiest people in the computer industry—not to mention the world!—earned most of their money in start-ups. The excitement of working on a new product, the greater control and responsibility one usually has in a start-up, and the more intimate working atmosphere of most start-ups can be almost as attractive as the potential monetary rewards. A start-up also can be a disastrous venture for all concerned. For each start-up that succeeds, many more quietly fail, leaving their employees without jobs.

---

work. In *Technology Review,* David Talbot describes the work of one researcher, Rolf Isermann, as "developing software that detects combustion misfires, which can damage catalytic converters and add to pollution."[44] Computer and electronic engineers are working on other projects in the field of mechatronics. Embedded systems is another area of technological development that will lead to more jobs for engineers. This technology is a way of putting computers in devices that are not computers in order to automate them. Embedded technology is used in cell phones and appliances such as microwaves.

While the Bureau of Labor Statistics projects a faster-than-average growth in the number of jobs (64 percent between 2000 and 2010), hardware engineers were not so optimistic in 2003. This is because one in five lost jobs in the previous few years, and not all of them were able to find other jobs with comparable duties and salaries. Still, when reporting these job losses, Adam Martin—in *Business2.0,* an online journal—predicts a turnaround. While he reports that more than 20 percent of computer hardware employees lost their jobs between 2000 and 2003, on a more hopeful note, he predicts that the trend will ultimately be upward because "all that hardware in use will have to be replaced or upgraded."[45]

Chapter 4

Video Game Designers

Video game designers are responsible for creating and designing video games. These include games that people play on consoles (an electrical box that connects to a television), arcade machines, computers, cell phones, and other electronic devices generally referred to as platforms. The common element among video games on all platforms is that they have a screen that displays the game action and a way for the player to control the game, either with a keyboard, joystick, or the keys on a cell phone. Game designers work on different types of games depending on who has hired them to make the game. For instance, if a designer works for a computer company, he or she will design games for computers. Increasingly in the twenty-first century, each game will be made for more than one platform.

Designers may work more or less independently, taking care of programming, animation, and production, including music and sound effects. However, designers on large, commercial projects typically work as part of a team that includes, at a minimum, programmers (who have C++ and 3D animation expertise), a producer (who oversees the business aspects of the project and coordinates the activities of the team), artists, and animators. In fact, designers typically start out in one of these areas, and after gaining experience and doing an endless amount of networking, move on to become designers.

Deciding on the Type of Game

Video game designers begin by coming up with an idea for a game they believe has promise, then gradually work out the extensive details required to bring that idea to life. Those details include the game's characters, the situations that will challenge the players, how the game will look, and what kind of sound effects or music will be used to add excitement. There are many types of video games. For instance, games may require players to take characters through a maze or may have good characters and bad characters pitted against one another in fights or other tests of skill. Games may be sports games, for instance, where a player plays on a basketball team or drives a race car. One type of game that is becoming hugely popular in the twenty-first century is the role-playing game (RPG), which allows users to become characters in games that have complex plots.

Because games vary greatly, a designer's first job is to decide what kind of game they wish to design. There is no science to this process; in fact, imagining a video game is a creative process that cannot be taught. Ideas may come from an experience the designer has had, from a desire to expand on another designer's idea, or

Shigeru Miyamoto is a video game designer for Nintendo. Video game designers usually work on an individual basis.

from other sources, many of which are never articulated by designers. These points are well illustrated by Toru Iwatani, designer of Pac-Man, one of the most famous video games of the twentieth century. He described the evolution of the game to Susan Lammers for her book *Programmers at Work, Interviews with 19 Programmers Who Shaped the Computer Industry:*

Two Animation Techniques

In order to make characters in video games move, animators use different types of animation, sometimes in combination with each other. In one type, called frame-based animation, animators create a series of frames with each showing the same background and image. To make the image move they insert small graphic changes (such as a slightly lower chin to show a character nodding) in each frame. When viewed in succession at certain speeds these frames create the illusion of continuous movement. In "sprite," or cast, animation (so-called because it mimics cast members in a play moving around a stationary stage) animators create a static background then move the images or characters (sprites) across the background. In Sams Teach Yourself Game Programming in 24 Hours, Michael Morrison explains the difference between these two types of animation and how both are used in a typical video game:

A good example of how games often require the use of more than one animation technique is an animation of a person walking. You obviously need to be able to alter the position of the person so that he appears to be moving across a landscape. This requires cast-based animation because you need to move the person independently of the background on which he appears. However, if we let it go at this, the person would appear to just be sliding across the screen because he isn't making any movements that simulate walking. To effectively simulate walking, the person needs to move his arms and legs like a real person does when walking. This requires frame-based animation because you need to show a series of frames of the leg and arm movements. The end result is an object that can both move and change its appearance, which is where the two animation techniques come together.

First of all, the [Japanese] word "taberu," to eat, came to mind. Game design, you see, often begins with words. I started playing with the word, making sketches in my notebook. All the computer games available at the time were of the violent type—war games and space invader types. There were no games that everyone could enjoy, and especially none for women. I wanted to come up with a "comical" game women could enjoy. The story I like to tell about the origin of Pac Man is that one lunch time I was quite hungry and I ordered a whole pizza. I helped myself to a wedge and what was left was the idea for the Pac Man shape.[46]

Working Out the Details

The type of game a designer chooses will guide every detail of the design process. While designers of action games propel players onward by requiring quick reflexes and little thought, designers of games with more subtle elements—such as Tenchu, which uses stealth action—take a different approach. For example, players who find themselves in potentially devastating circumstances may not get an immediate "game over" signal, but instead have a brief moment to escape. This allows the game to continue instead of creating what designer Tad Horie calls a "trial-and-error process,"[47] which forces users to keep starting over when unable to get out of a life or death situation.

Once a designer knows the type of game they wish to design, they begin working on the myriad of details that must be established. Every action in the game must be defined. For instance, the designer decides if a character will be able to jump over objects and, if so, how high. Decisions are made about how fast a character moves, what kind of opposition will be encountered, and how many chances a player gets to beat that opposition before they "die" (lose the round of play). Justin Quimby designs and writes programs for online games called massively multiplayer online (MMO), so-called because they allow many people to play simultaneously online. Explaining some of the technical aspects of his job, Quimby says: "We create three-dimensional worlds where hundreds of thousands of people from all around the world adventure and socialize together. Basically, I define the rules . . . of the game world. For example, I code how much dam-age a sword swing does or how a monster will react to seeing a player peek around a corner."[48]

Making It Fun and Lasting

In deciding on the details of a game, designers spend a great deal of time considering how to make it fun and how to keep the play-er coming back to the game over and over. This aspect of game design involves an intuitive mastery of how appealing the look and feel of a game will be, how much drama and excitement there is, and, thus, how users will interact with what they see on the screen. To understand why this is so important, it is helpful to consider the difference between video game entertainment and other forms of visual entertainment, such as cartoons. In car-toons, viewers watch what is happening but do not have a physi-cal or mental role that influences the outcome. Video games are quite different, as online writer and designer Bob Rafei explains: "[One] major attribute of games is that it requires an *active* versus *passive* audience participation. No two players will have the exact same experience playing the exact same game. . . . If the player doesn't like the feel of the controls or the play mechanics, the best-crafted story sequences will not save the game."[49] Video game designers are always conscious of the importance of creat-ing a positive interactive experience, one that the player wants to return to. Their approach will vary depending on the type of game. For instance, speed may be all-important in a maze game, while a more subtle approach is required for other types of games.

To create a fun game, designers balance technology with artistry, meaning they accomplish their entertainment goals within the limits of programs and the platforms for which they are designing. For example, because working with wireless games on a small cell phone screen means having less "real estate" (screen space) than is available on a laptop or console video screen, designers take a different approach, not only when decid-ing on the programs to use to code the game, but also when con-ceptualizing the action. Ralph Barbagallo, who founded a video game studio, explains that the skills needed to make great games on this medium are somewhat unique: "It's actually good if some-one has early video game experience because for wireless games they need many of the same skills—how to tell a compelling story with few pixels [dots that make up an image on the screen] and small amounts of memory."[50]

Keeping a game interesting even as players advance through the different levels is another task for designers. In one RPG game called True Fantasy Live Online, in development for the online version of XBox, players can become a fantasy character by choosing props, clothes, looks (including whether to be an elf or have wild-looking hair), and careers. Because RPG games can become stagnant after many hours of play, chief designer Akihiro Hino has three designers hard at work to map out the details of the characters' work lives by developing time lines, as he explains, "to see what happens within the first 10 hours, what happens during the following 10, what happens between hours 100 to 150."[51] Through this method, he hopes to create roles that will never lose their freshness.

An Unnameable Quality

Designers often have a knack for or intense interest in one type of game over another. This is one factor that leads to a conclusion that game design—which relies so much on the creative juices of individual designers—is the most personal of computer careers. Thus, even those designers who have excellent training in programming so they understand the medium and how to use it to its maximum capacity may not succeed. Bill Roper, one of the most famous designers of the twentieth century, explains how important individual talent is for the success of games: "It's the people who make the games. Just like you want Stephen King or J.K. Rowling to be writing your book, you want the best possible people making a game for you."[52]

Whatever their artistic vision, game designers must keep up with changing technology. Video game designers of the twenty-first century will continue to develop games that can be played on computers, and on consoles such as Playstation 2 (made by Sony). However, in Sams Teach Yourself Game Programming in 24 Hours, Michael Morrison points out that even this technology is evolving into one that may well allow consoles to take center stage in home entertainment:

We are currently in the midst of a convergence of digital entertainment technologies that is quite capable of placing console games at the center of the home entertainment equation. In fact, Microsoft already has long range plans for its XBox console game system to become an all-encompassing digital entertainment device. The next few years should be interesting in terms of seeing how console games merge with traditional entertainment equipment.[53]

A woman enjoys playing a video game on her home computer. Video game designers are exceedingly creative individuals with a talent for creating fun and exciting games.

Competing with Movies

Technology has evolved to the point where video game designers can create images that begin to rival those seen in the movies. However, commentators caution that those two mediums are far from identical and that even when they have impressive graphics as tools, video game designers have a great challenge: They must create a story that keeps the user interested enough to return to it over and over again. Nevertheless, game designers of the twenty-first century will vie with moviemakers for the attention of increasingly demanding audiences. In "The Play's the Thing, but . . ." for *Computer Graphics World*, Bill Kovacs describes the efforts of game designers in this regard: "They are in pursuit of larger budgets, more challenging stories, and, in short, anything that brings a more satisfying experience to an increasingly broad game market." In fact, production of big commercial games takes a great deal of money, often millions of dollars, and one to three years to complete.

Because their work is both limited and broadened by technology, game designers have highly analytical minds. They fit together the various pieces of the technological puzzle to create a satisfying entertainment experience. This means always being conscious of the limits of the technology—from how much memory is available to how elaborate images can become without slowing down the action. Designers have a fascination for the industry because they are constantly called upon to react to business developments brought about by new technologies. For instance, designers interested in the wireless market meet the needs of both telecommunications companies, which may have content requirements such as no violence, and of customers, who have a variety of platforms that require the use of different programs, many of which are evolving very quickly.

Not Always Glamorous

Because there is so much technical work involved, designers cannot always focus solely on the excitement and fun of developing games. They also do tedious work that includes dealing with any glitches in the program and documenting the process of developing the game. Even so, there are far more people who want to become designers than will actually make it. Besides its competitive nature, the video game design field has another significant negative: The market for new games fluctuates a great deal, making demand for designers highly variable. In addition, video game production companies come and go or are gobbled up by bigger companies that may no longer need the services of the old company's employees. Darryl S. Duncan, a composer and musician who owns a company that produces sound effects and music for video games, has this to say about the uncertainty of staying in one job in this industry: "The rise and fall of various game designers is sort of scary for someone deciding to move across the country to accept a particular position. . . . I have many colleagues that change companies almost every two years, and some are out of work because many startups fail and many established companies downsize."[54]

In spite of these challenges, those who become video game designers consider themselves to be extremely lucky. Designers find their work stimulating, varied, creative, and unique among jobs in the computer field. As the twenty-first century progresses, designers are being swept along with a tide created by technological developments that allow far more complexity, sophistication, and speed than ever before—factors that many designers find exciting. They enjoy the creative challenge, the variety, and the opportunity to express their visions in a cutting-edge medium. As Morrison points out, "No matter how fancy the graphics are or how immersive the sound, the overriding design goal of any game is always to maximize fun. Who wouldn't want to spend all day trying to figure out the best way to have fun?"[55]

College Not Required

Game designers follow many different educational paths to get to their dream job. At the dawn of the twenty-first century, a college degree was not a requirement, although certain employers like to see a degree, even if they are not concerned with what the degree is in. The book *50 Cutting-Edge Jobs* (published in 2000) lists just one school that has a game design degree, DigiPen, which is located in Redmond, Washington. However, as technology continues to make inroads into college programs, video game designers will increasingly compete with others who have taken courses in their field.

Mastering one of the entry careers—producer, programmer, or animator—is considered by many experts the best way to get into the business of designing video games. Game testers and others willing to do grunt work for game companies may find themselves making connections that will help them move into a job producing games. Producers take care of the business end, including budgeting, and the coordination of projects. Programmers need to be experts in 3D programming and other languages essential to the industry. This means keeping up with changes in the most popular applications. Animators and artists need to be able to draw and to show a sample video of their work. Writing, math, and good communication skills are necessary no matter where game designers start.

Having a passion for playing games and for all things related to playing games, such as tinkering with new programs, attending

Pixar Animation Studios executive Ralph Guggenheim (right) poses with one of his animators. Video game designers typically start out as animators, producers, or programmer.

Video Games Imitating Life

Designers of the twenty-first century are increasingly moving toward games that, instead of being based on competition, more closely mirror the complexities and subtleties of real life. The trend is toward allowing for social interaction, not only through the vehicle of the massively multiplayer online (MMO) game, but also by basing games on people's experiences living and working together rather than fighting or competing. In reviewing the game Star Wars: Knights of the Old Republic, Evan Shamoon, editor-in-chief of XBN magazine, commented on this recently recognized potential for games, saying that Knights of the Old Republic makes people think about their choices in the game and, as an extension of that, makes players "draw conclusions applicable to real life."

trade shows, and reading print and online magazines such *Cinefex, American Cinematographer, Graphics World,* and *3D Design,* is a good start toward getting a foot in the door. Having an innate sense of what makes a game good from the players' standpoint is also essential. But as the website for the online recruiter CoolGameJobs.com explains, just being a fan of games is not enough to land a game designer title. Paying one's dues in one of the other jobs on the development team and honing one's communication skills are first steps. In addition, CoolGameJobs.com advises aspiring game designers to "learn everything you can about how games are put together. No one will hire you because 'you have a great idea for a new game.' . . . Pretty much everyone who loves games enough to want to make them for a living has a great idea for a new game."[56]

Potential Earnings

For those willing to learn the field, game design can be lucrative. CoolGameJobs.com reports that while game programmers earn $45,000 to $55,000 a year, the top designers make $150,000 to $250,000. Experienced producers who can handle large projects make $80,000 to $100,000, while the highest level executive producers earn over $100,000. Artists and animators start in the $50,000 to $60,000 range and can make over $100,000 at the highest levels.

A Blossoming Industry

While the video game industry rises and falls and game companies come and go, the early years of the twenty-first century are expected to be promising and lucrative for those who have the skills that development companies need. In fact, because of the growth associated with complex games, which need far bigger development teams, game companies are vying for qualified candidates and are paying excellent salaries. According to Khanh T.L. Tran in *CareerJournal.com*, "Business is blossoming as the [game] industry advances toward the peak of the five-year cycle for [consoles]."[57] The end of these cycles brings out new versions of hardware that in turn spurs new sales. Excellence, reliability, flexibility, and the continuing acquisition of new skills, especially those that allow one to do several of the jobs involved in making video games, are the best ways to protect a career in this field.

Chapter 5

Computer Technicians

Computer technicians install, maintain, and repair computers and related machines, such as printers and modems. They work in person, by phone, or by e-mail to help troubleshoot, diagnose, and fix problems. They have the skills to repair the physical and electrical components of a machine, but they are also well acquainted with the "intelligent" parts of the computer—the operating system (the program that oversees the computer's functioning) and software—because they also troubleshoot problems that these can cause.

Computer technicians' skills are needed in many different settings. Computer manufacturers, stores, and computer repair service companies employ computer technicians to make repairs that are required under a computer's original warranty or by an extended service contract, which a customer buys to lengthen the warranty coverage. In these situations, technicians may work at computer repair centers, remaining at the workbench ("bench technician") during the workday, or they may go to homes or businesses to make repairs and to install and maintain equipment. Technicians may work in-house for companies, educational institutions, and government agencies that need on-site personnel. They may also work for telecommunications companies, such as high-speed Internet companies, that need to make sure customers' computers are configured and maintained to accommodate the company's technology.

Diagnosing and Problem Solving

Problem solving is a key task of computer technicians, who begin by evaluating whether the problem is caused by broken equipment (hardware) or from an operating system or software failure. Author Harry Henderson summarizes typical hardware problems this way: "Hard drives . . . crash, monitors blow out, or a loose chip starts causing intermittent memory problems."[58] Problems other than those caused by hardware include a computer's failure to "boot up," the process by which the computer starts after clearing memory and loading the operating system.

To develop an understanding of the root of the trouble, technicians find out what led the user to call a technician by asking the user questions about what has gone wrong. They then examine the equipment to find any obvious problems, such as a disconnected cable or broken monitor. Oftentimes technicians need to conduct research to identify the problem. They read documentation that came with the computer and go online to manufacturers' websites. In some cases, they contact a support person at the hardware or software company. In her book *Upgrade and Repair with Jean Andrews*, Andrews, an expert on computer

Computer technicians install, maintain, and repair computers. They may work in person, by phone, or by e-mail to help troubleshoot and fix problems.

repairs, gives this specific example of the importance of also considering user error: "In [an] example of [a] problem with corrupted Word documents, the most obvious or simplest source of the problem is that the user is not saving documents properly. Eliminate that possibility before you look at the software or the hard drive as the source of the problem."[59]

Technicians use tools such as a multimeter (a handheld device with probes that can be attached to electrical devices to measure voltage) to find out what is wrong. They use troubleshooting programs to find out the source of nonhardware problems. To use these tools, they enter a complex series of commands that help reveal the source of the problem by, for instance, creating reports that show where a problem originated.

Throughout the process of diagnosis, technicians keep in mind that whatever is done to the computer can cause the user to lose data and programs. To the extent possible, technicians find ways of saving data—for instance, by backing it up onto floppy disks if there is enough functioning space on the computer to do so. During a repair visit, a technician may remind the user that this is a good habit to get into before a problem occurs.

Making Repairs

Once technicians learn the source of a breakdown, they take steps to fix the problem. At times the repair is completed by taking basic steps with basic equipment. For these instances, technician Joel Lutenberg offers the following advice: "Every computer technician should have a little tool set of screwdrivers and basic tools because you're going to have to open up computers and printers and other peripherals. A can of compressed air helps clean out dust and debris that accumulates inside a printer or a computer."[60]

Because many parts are inexpensive relative to the hourly cost of a technician, technicians often recommend replacing old or broken parts rather than repairing them. Technicians help obtain the new parts by contacting the manufacturer. Large companies may have separate purchasing departments that order new parts that the technician then installs.

Software tools used to diagnose operating system and other software-related problems are also used to repair those problems.

By inputting commands, technicians can cause the computer to complete a number of helpful steps—for instance, restoring lost data.

Preventing Problems

While technicians who work within a company spend a significant amount of time fixing computers, they are most effective when they have a plan to help minimize the need for repair. This means that they perform preventive maintenance on a regular basis. This includes a range of activities, such as cleaning dust out of the computer case with a small vacuum or can of compressed air and running battery tests. In addition, technicians set guidelines for computer users to make sure they do not inadvertently cause problems—for instance, by leaving drinks where they could spill onto computer equipment. Andrews describes the importance of a preventive maintenance program this way:

> If you are responsible for the PCs in an organization, make and implement a preventive maintenance plan to help prevent failures and reduce repair costs and downtime. . . . PC failures are caused by many different environmental and human factors, including heat, dust, magnetism, power supply problems, static electricity, human error (such as spilled liquids or an accidental change of setup and software configurations), and viruses. The goals of preventive maintenance are to reduce the likelihood that the events that cause PC failures will occur and to lessen the damage if they do occur.[61]

Uniqueness of Computer Repair

Because technicians encounter many problems relating to the operating system and software, the knowledge required for them to do their job well goes beyond what is typically thought of for those who repair machines. At the very least, beginning technicians learn to distinguish between a problem that could be caused by software, such as not having enough memory for the applications the user is trying to load, or a hardware problem such as a lack of power or a worn-out hard drive. As they develop experience, technicians have a much more sophisticated command of how to use software and operating system diagnostic and repair tools.

Low-Tech Jobs

While technicians enjoy their work because it is technical in nature, not all workers in the computer technology field have to be technically inclined. In High-Tech Careers for Low-Tech People, *author William A. Schaffer explains how people with nontechnical backgrounds, such as those with marketing experience or with journalism degrees, can find work in the computer industry. The book lists a number of low-tech jobs, including those in sales, human resources, project coordinating, public relations, and marketing. This excerpt includes a few of Schaffer's suggestions to help those without computer expertise look for jobs with high-tech companies:*

Getting a [low-tech] job in high tech is almost always the result of a process that you initiate and execute, and over which you have control. . . . In part, getting into high tech is a numbers game: the more possibilities you uncover, the greater the chances you'll find your first high-tech job. In large part, too, it's a connections game—a game of networking, if you prefer that term. Some people consider *networking* to be an overworked term, but it's a very powerful tool. . . . Effective communication is an essential element as well. We low-tech people have the raw material to enable us to be good communicators. In the hiring interviews we must demonstrate not only how smart, energetic, and articulate we are, but also that we can listen thoughtfully to others, ask sensible questions, and generally build empathy with the interviewers. Finally, the job hunt involves quite a bit of methodical work—to uncover those opportunities, to learn about the histories, products, technologies, finances, employees, and cultures of the companies you target.

The mental ability to systematically diagnose problems is essential, but computer technicians also have certain physical quatlities. A good dose of manual dexterity is essential because they manipulate small parts. At the same time, however, they are strong enough to lift and move heavy equipment without becoming injured.

Obvious, but worth mentioning, is that technicians enjoy learning about new technologies. They are also willing to tackle whatever comes their way, and that can be a dizzying task, not only because of the variety of equipment and technologies, but also because many offices and homes still have computers that contain older components. For instance, the motherboard is an extremely important part of a computer, and it is one that comes in many different vintages, sizes, and layouts.

A Little Bit Mind Reader

In addition to their technical skills, technicians are good communicators, because gaining information from users is essential to making the right diagnosis. However, in many instances, basic interpersonal skills are not enough; technicians need to be a little bit psychologist and a little bit mind reader, especially when dealing with home computer users. Helping customers over the phone puts technicians' skills to a real test because they are required to visualize what is happening without the advantage of

Because computer technicians often work with complex computer hardware like this one, they must have a strong working knowledge of advanced diagnostic and repair tools.

being hands-on. Also, they must deal with the individual person-alities of users. For instance, some customers cannot describe the kind of equipment or software they have, some are terrified of using computers and have a hard time following a technician's instructions, and some want to chitchat about any topic under the sun. Technicians have the ability to understand what type of person they are dealing with and respond accordingly. Even those technicians with good interpersonal skills may find it challenging to deal with customers who believe they know more than the technician does. Andrews, a computer science professor, address-es these issues in her book *Upgrade and Repair with Jean Andrews:*

> Sometimes a customer is proud of what he or she knows about computers. This type of customer may want to give advice, take charge of a call, withhold information that he or she thinks you don't need to know, or execute com-mands at the computer without letting you know, so that you don't have enough information to follow along. A sit-uation like this must be handled with tact and respect for the customer. . . . When you can, compliment the cus-tomer concerning his or her knowledge, experience, or insight. . . . Use technical language in a way that conveys that you expect the customer to understand you.[62]

Injuries and Sometimes Isolation

Working with customers who are in a computer crisis can wear a technician down. Also, in jobs that require twenty-four-hour sup-port, irregular hours can be taxing. Technicians who work at the bench or in the field have limited opportunities to establish working relationships with colleagues because they are physically isolated or on the go from one place to another. Some technicians complain that they do not have good advancement opportunities or that their pay is low. In addition, because much of the techni-cians' work is physical, they may experience injuries, such as minor cuts from sharp parts, electrical shocks, or back strain from moving heavy equipment.

Technicians who do not like the isolation associated with bench work may enjoy working in-house. This situation has advantages for people who want to get to know and interact with

Tinkering

After warning that computers are electrical devices and that open-ing them without proper precautions can be dangerous, Drew Bird and Mike Harwood, authors of Information Technology Careers: The Hottest Jobs for the New Millennium, *suggest that tinker-ing at home may be one of the best ways for aspiring computer tech-nicians to learn about how the meshing of hardware, software, and operating systems makes computers work:*

If you want to get some hands-on practice without risking cost-ly accidents, consider purchasing a used computer that can become a test-bed for your experiments. A system that is nei-ther cutting edge, nor rusting away, is perfect. In many cases, such a unit is quite representative of what you may end up dealing with in the field. If funds are tight, consider approaching local computer stores and asking them for old PC equipment, or even place a want ad in your local newspaper. Although this strategy may cause you to end up with a reasonable amount of junk, you may just find enough components to build a system. In fact, the older and weirder the components you get, the more likely they are to represent a challenge in configuration and setup. By experimenting with these types of components and troubleshooting the conflicts, you will learn a great deal more than if the system was complete at the outset.

coworkers instead of interacting with strangers most of the time. An in-house technician may be seen as a friend by fellow cowork-ers because the work involves more than coming to the rescue in a crisis (and possibly not having an immediate solution in cases where parts must be ordered). Coworkers appreciate technicians who arrive in their offices with a big box holding new equipment that they cheerfully set up and make operational.

Learning by Doing

Computer technicians do not need four-year college degrees. Instead, they receive training through several other avenues. One is through apprenticeship programs sponsored by a company or agency. Here, the technician works on the job under the supervision of more experienced technicians and takes courses such as electronics and programming to complement the practical side of the training. Workers appreciate apprenticeship opportunities because they allow them to start learning and start earning at least a modest salary right away.

Another way technicians train is through certification programs sponsored by associations such as the Computing Technology Industry Association (CompTIA) or the International Society of Certified Electronics Technicians (ISCET). On its website, the ISCET explains why their program is valuable not only to technicians, but also to businesses and consumers who have no other way to judge the qualifications of those who work on equipment that is vital to both: "The Certification Program can help assure consumers that the person entrusted to service their electronic products possesses the knowledge, the training and the experience necessary to do a good job."[63]

Technicians may also get an associate degree, which is awarded after the completion of about twenty classes that include not only highly technical subjects, but also more general ones in English and math. In "Associate Degree: Two Years to a Career or a Jump Start to a Bachelor's Degree" from the *Occupational Outlook Quarterly*, Olivia Crosby gives this advice for selecting an associate degree program: "The best programs tailor courses to industry standards. Schools ask local employers what skill workers need to perform specific occupations. Then, the schools create classes that teach those skills. With the help of advisors from local businesses, curriculums are updated regularly."[64]

Once they finish training and begin working, technicians keep current with technologies by reading information about products released by manufacturers, websites with updated information, and magazines and journals. This is an important part of the technician's job, because not every service call that is made will involve a problem that the technician has handled before. Learning on the job is a process that can continue for months or years. While employers expect a certain level of skill from those who have completed the different training and education avenues, they do not typically hand the most complex jobs over to new workers. Instead, as explained in the *Occupational Outlook Handbook*, technicians advance this way: "Newly hired computer repairers may work on personal computers or peripheral equipment. With experience, they can advance to positions maintaining more sophisticated systems, such as networking equipment and servers."[65]

As a result of the rapid pace of technological change, computer technicians must continuously learn on the job.

Technician Skills Are Useful in Related Careers

Those who become expert computer technicians but who decide not to stay in this career may use their expertise to move into related areas. For instance, becoming a computer or computer parts salesperson may be a good fit for an outgoing technician who enjoys the challenge of earning a living that is partially based on commissions. Technicians may also move from fixing computers to working at a company's help desk. In this function, they answer phone and e-mail questions from workers. For instance, they may explain how to log on or how to send an e-mail attachment. Technicians who develop an excellent understanding of the technical requirements of networking computers may take courses in networking and computer science that will allow them to move into careers as network administrators.

Income and Employment Potential

While many technicians stay in and enjoy these positions, the relatively low pay compared to most other computer-related jobs may discourage some people from making a lifelong commitment to repairing computers. Computer technicians in the year 2000 earned a median hourly wage of $15.05, or approximately $30,000 a year. While some made as little as $9.50 an hour, the highest paid made more than $23.42 an hour. In order to earn more money, some technicians may go into business for themselves. Others may become managers, and still others may move into related fields, such as programming or sales. Those who rise to supervisory levels oversee the work of and hire less experienced technicians, give advice, and help resolve the more difficult technical problems. They also become involved in keeping track of employee schedules and budgeting for new equipment and repair tools.

The Bureau of Labor Statistics overestimated the increase in the number of technician jobs from 1988 to 2000, and economists Andrew Alpert and Jill Auyer suggest that perhaps fewer companies than expected increased their use of computers or that "equipment improvements led to fewer breakdowns."[66] Thus, the Bureau of Labor Statistics modified the expected growrh for these careers from much faster than average (31 percent or more) to about as fast as average (a predicted 11–19 percent). Still, since computers are now used in virtually every office setting and the technician's skills are essential to maintaining optimal operating capacity, aspiring technicians should have plenty of opportunities for satisfying employment.

Chapter 6

Web Developers

Web developers are responsible for creating and maintaining websites and Web pages (the individual screens that appear on a website). On the technical side, their duties include coding and programming to make a website available to the public on the Internet or to allow employees within a company to connect to each other's computers via an intranet. Web developers also design and implement tools that allow users to navigate the pages of a website or to complete some action, such as ordering merchandise from an on-line seller (an e-commerce site). Web developers also handle the nontechnical tasks necessary to create a website. These include writing the content (text) and designing graphics to make the site appealing. Other important tasks include monitoring the site to see how often it is being accessed and the kind of activity taking place. This allows the developer to determine if modifications are needed. Keeping the site up-to-date by incorporating content changes and deleting obsolete links (text or an image that users click on to take them to another page or site) is also a job of developers. In the twenty-first century, individual developers are likely to specialize in one or more Web development tasks, completing them as part of a Web development team.

Web developers work in many different settings. They may be freelancers, providing services on a contract basis, or employees of businesses, organizations, governmental agencies, and educational institutions. They also work for companies that specialize in developing and maintaining websites for other companies and individuals.

Planning Usable Sites

Web development includes many different types of tasks, which may be completed by one individual or by a team of people whose members become experts in one or more of those tasks, such as design (planning graphic impact), content (writing and editing

Some Web developers, like Ron Morris of Starwave, work as employees for large companies, while other Web developers freelance their services.

73

text), or programming. A Web developer's job may be combined with or separate from what some people call the webmaster function, which includes updating sites and responding to e-mail help requests from users. Creating a usable site is the core goal of designing websites, as described by the World Organization of Webmasters (WOW): "Usability is about ensuring that the site we design and develop is both useful and usable for its intended audience. It must be accessible, appealing, easy to learn, consistent, clear, memorable, efficient, navigable, and easy for the user to recover themselves if and when they make an error."[67]

While usability is a general goal, Web developers are also charged with meeting the specific aims of the site's sponsor. For instance, a caterer may simply want to display contact information, such as phone number and e-mail, and a sample menu that can be reached through a link from the home page (the main page of the site). However, a news website will be far more complex because its purpose is to provide up-to-the-minute information that is useful to people who visit the site from all over the country. Thus, this type of site will typically have dozens of links (to specific articles, for instance) and interactive tools. These tools allow users to customize the information received. For instance, they can input a zip code to receive a weather report for the user's hometown. E-commerce sites include product information and allow customers to select and purchase items.

The nature of a site sponsor's business provides helpful insight into the type of site a developer will create. However, to better understand the many details that go into finalizing a site—from how much animation will appear on a home page to whether to include a site map (an electronic table of contents)—developers consult with representatives of the sponsor company, including marketing personnel. Developers also attend meetings with others on the Web development team to brainstorm and reach decisions about the best way to proceed. Throughout the planning process, Web developers are conscious of the user's interaction (interface) with a site. Thus, developers consider how easy it is to put items into an electronic shopping cart (a separate page that lists items the customer is considering buying) or whether the home page is so cluttered with graphics that a user will become confused.

Selecting Tools and Coding with HTML

Once the purpose is outlined, developers decide which tool or tools to use to create the website. These tools include codes and programs that allow developers to input the site's text, graphics, animation, sound, and links in such a way that they can be accessed and used by anyone whose computer has a compatible browser (a Web navigation program such as Netscape Navigator or Internet Explorer). To define how pages should look and to delineate links to other pages within the site (or to other websites), developers often use hypertext markup language (HTML), a system of codes or tags that mark the beginning and end of a style, such as bold or italics, the location of a link, and the background graphics. The authors of *Creating Web Pages All-in-One Desk Reference for Dummies* use the following example of how developers use HTML coding to create a page that, when opened by the user's browser, will appear to have a background graphic of fleas covered by text reading "With a scratcha scratcha here and a scratcha scratcha there:" "<BODY **BACKGROUND= "flea.gif"**> With a scratcha scratcha here and a scratcha scratcha there </BODY>."[68] In this example, the code is used to signify the page's beginning and end (note the "/" for end in the second BODY command) and designates that the graphic of fleas will be the background.

In addition to HTML, Web developers use programs such as PaintShop Pro, Java, and Flash to add graphics, sound, and video to the site. Developers of e-commerce sites use additional tools to allow credit card information to be transmitted securely and to connect the website to databases that contain information about the availability of products.

Because computer technology continually evolves, Web developers spend time reading online and print magazines to find the best products to aid in the design process and in the execution of the site. They look for new products by keeping in touch with others in the field and by reading ads and reviews that appear in computer magazines and journals or online. For example, the WOW website includes evaluations of products that can help improve the quality of graphics or make the design process more efficient. Web developers also attend courses sponsored by software companies, colleges, and technical schools and associations to learn about emerging technologies.

Complying with Federal Law

Companies whose websites are aimed at, or which the company knows are used by, children under thirteen years old must comply with the federal Children's Online Privacy Protection Act. Thus, developers must be aware of the requirements of the act when they design websites. This excerpt from a brochure entitled How to Comply with the Children's Online Privacy Protection Act, a Guide from the Federal Trade Commission, the Direct Marketing Association, and the Internet Alliance, *explains the notice provisions of the act:*

An operator must post a link to a notice of its information practices on the home page of its Web site or online service *and* at each area where it collects personal information from children. An operator of a general audience site with a separate children's area must post a link to its notice on the home page of the children's area. The link to the privacy notice must be clear and prominent. Operators may want to use a larger font size or a different color type on a contrasting background to make it stand out. A link in small print at the bottom of the page—or a link that is indistinguishable from other links on your site—is not considered clear and prominent.

Understanding Their Audience

While they enjoy the stimulation of learning about new technologies, developers do not use the most advanced methods just because they find them personally appealing. Instead, they consider the impact of their technology choices on the intended users. Because users have different types of computers (platforms) and different browsers and versions of those browsers (e.g., Netscape Navigator 4.0), coding and programming that works well for one user may not work well—or at all—for others. In *Web Design in a Nutshell, a Desktop Quick Reference*, author and computer expert Jennifer Niederst provides helpful guidance to Web developers trying to decide which technologies to use:

Most web authors agree that the biggest challenge (and headache!) in web design is dealing with the variety of browsers and platforms. . . . Features and capabilities improve with each new major browser release, but that doesn't mean the older versions just go away. . . . How do you design web pages that are [visually] and technically intriguing without alienating those in your audience with older browsers? Does a page that is designed to be functional on all browsers necessarily need to be boring? Is it possible to please everyone? And if not, where do you draw the line? . . . There's no absolute rule here. . . . The key to making appropriate design decisions lies in understanding your audience and considering how your site is going to be used.[69]

A website for a public library may have users with slow computers that cannot handle the large amount of data required to transmit graphics. Thus, a Web developer for this site may concentrate on the text and avoid trying to make the design too elaborate. On the other hand, a company trying to sell expensive, modern furniture may use a Flash animation presentation to entice customers, but allow those users without Flash technology on their computers to select a simpler presentation.

Testing and Publishing a Site

Once a website is ready to launch, Web developers determine the best way to make it available and accessible to the masses of people who use the Internet. At this stage, Web developers may be involved in a number of different steps to complete the process of publishing the site, including testing, using programming software to upload the site to a server, picking and reserving a domain name (the name people type in to access the site), and registering the site with search engines, such as Google and Lycos, that publicize and include links to the site.

Testing is important because mistakes can be made in coding HTML, for example, or the quirks of individual browsers may make the completed page look or work differently from what the developer intended. To test a site, developers can send their sites online to a validation service, which looks for errors in coding and shows how the site will look on different browsers. Developers can also test their sites by uploading them to the Internet and opening the site using a variety of computers and

An IBM spokesperson announces the release of a new online security system. Prior to launch, all websites are thoroughly tested by Web developers.

browsers. However, this can cause a problem because once the site is published on the Internet, anyone can access it. To avoid having a stranger find the site while it is still in the testing stage, a developer will use special software that allows their computer to mimic an Internet setting but not allow access from the outside.

Keeping an Eye Out

For several reasons, Web developers keep a watchful eye over their creations. One reason is that websites are linked together, and the sites that users go to from the developer's site may become obsolete, either because they cease to exist or because the information contained in them is no longer useful. For instance, an entertainment site that is sponsoring a poll to predict which movies will win Oscars might contain a link to other sites that include movie reviews. Once the Academy Awards are bestowed for that year, users of the site may have less interest in those reviews and may instead be interested in linking to the websites of the winners of awards, thus creating the need for the developer to update the site. In addition, sites come and go, and developers do not want their users to receive error messages when they try to link; therefore, developers periodically check links to make sure they still exist. Checking links may occur daily or less frequently, depending on the type of site and the sponsor's site maintenance budget. Web developers work long hours to manage the content of their sites. For instance, pages that include ratings for movies, or an e-commerce site that sells merchandise that will change with the season or go on sale at different prices, are high maintenance.

The authors of *Creating Web Pages All-in-One Desk Reference for Dummies* emphasize that twenty-first-century users have become sophisticated enough to have little patience with sites that are not updated in a timely and professional way, meaning that the once-accepted "under construction" notice is a thing of the past:

An Amazing Development

The explosion of e-commerce at the end of the twentieth century changed the way companies do business and created many opportunities for Web developers that are expected to last well into the twenty-first century. James J. Hobuss explains in Building Sybase Web Sites *the importance of such sites in conducting business:*

On the Web, you can make a sales presentation or put promotional material in the hands of interested people at any hour of the day or night. Orders can be taken and product queued for shipment before your first cup of coffee in the morning. You no longer have to pony up the $3,000 to $4,000 it costs to send a salesperson around the world to meet with customers, although this is not to say that business travel for sales purposes can be eliminated by the Web. What this *is* saying is that with the Web, and the Internet, your company has the ability to interact with customers and potential customers in a format where geography and time have no relevance. When you do business on the Web, you have increased the accessibility to your customers, and from your customers.

For an e-commerce site, the correct approach isn't to apologize for not keeping your site up-to-date; it's to spend the time and effort required to keep your site up-to-date. Why? Because potential customers surfing an outdated e-commerce site may well assume that the company is no longer in business; at the very least, they assume that the company isn't particularly detail-oriented—not a good perception when you're trying to get their money![70]

Overseeing a site also includes checking on the way the site is being used, an important indicator of how effective the site is for its intended purpose. For instance, if customers are browsing on an e-commerce site but not buying anything, the developer may consider whether the site should be redesigned to make ordering easier.

A Range of Skills

Considering the range of their responsibilities, it is no wonder that Web developers have many different personal qualities and professional skills. For instance, they work independently but at the same time communicate well with many different kinds of people. They deftly handle meetings with a marketing director if they are working on an e-commerce site or with a politician's staff if they are creating a home page for someone running for office. Since they may be working on only one part of the development process, they work well with team members with complementary skills, including programmers and graphic designers. Web developers also work well within their organization, meeting deadlines and acting consistently with the organization's policies. For instance, a developer working at a university might promote the institution's policy of encouraging minority applicants by making sure that images presented on the site show students of different ethnicities.

Web developers possess a number of other different skills, from creativity to the ability to think logically and to solve problems. They look at their work as a user would, putting aside their own expertise and insider view of a site to see if it meets usability tests. They are also able to understand and follow laws that apply to their sites. For instance, the Children's Online Privacy Protection Act governs how websites collect and use information from children, requiring developers to post special notices on cer-

A team of Web developers meets to discuss projects. Because Web developers often work in teams, they must complement their technical skills with strong personal skills.

tain websites. In order to comply with copyright laws, developers obtain permission from those who own the copyright for the text, graphics, and sound they wish to use. In *Web Design in a Nutshell, a Desktop Quick Reference*, Niederst gives an example pertaining to developers who are considering using audio (sound) files on their sites:

> Like images, there are a number of sources for acquiring audio files to use on a web site. Be aware, however, simply posting somebody else's music or recordings from a CD is a copyright violation. Record companies and entertainment corporations are taking measures to crack down on the illegal use of copyrighted material. Even collections of silly sound effects that seem like they were designed for multiple uses may be protected. Be sure to read the fine print for terms of use.[71]

Websites are technology and information driven, and in the twenty-first century, this means constant change. Thus, Web developers face the challenge of keeping current with technologies, such as improved animation software, that allow them to create sites that are competitive with other sponsors' sites. In addition, Web developers often work under stress in order to meet development deadlines and handle emergencies, such as a site crash. Depending on the area of focus, Web development requires excellent writing and organizing abilities, a keen sense of design, and a mastery of several different programs and codes.

An Evolution in Training

While Web developers of the twenty-first century are less likely to handle all aspects of website development and implementation, working in Web development requires understanding of and proficiency in not only the artistic and entertainment aspects of developing websites, but also in the technical methods necessary to get designs onto the screens of users. Preparation to become a Web developer varies depending on the focus of the developer's career. It was more common in the twentieth century for developers to start out working informally, creating personal home pages for themselves, friends, or family members. Those pages then became part of a portfolio to help Web developers find jobs in businesses or with Web development companies. One experienced intranet developer explains the informal way in which some in her career got started in this area:

> One way to start out in this field is as an intern. You take a couple of classes in graphic design and learn how to use Photoshop. And learn how to use HTML. You've got to have a good eye for how information is organized. That's what it really boils down to. A couple of my friends have gone from waiting tables to learning the basics of some office productivity packages out there, when they did temp work.[72]

In the twenty-first century, more colleges are offering courses that relate to Web development, and this will most likely create an expectation that those who wish to enter the field have degrees, or at least concentrations in subjects that relate specifically to that field. In the twentieth century, typical undergraduate degrees for those focusing on website design included visual arts and graphic design. However, those with more specialized degrees in user interface design or information design, for example, will have a competitive edge, provided that they do not rely solely on college training but continuously update their skills to master new technologies.

While the specialties evolve quickly, in the earliest years of the twenty-first century, the most basic work in Web development required excellent skill in HTML and JavaScript (a programming language for interactive websites) and familiarity with JPEG and GIF (formats that reduce the amount of memory used by pictures). Those who seek to specialize in layout are now expected to have mastered the most popular programs, including Dreamweaver, GoLive, and Front Page. Multimedia experts will benefit from outstanding skills in programs such as Shockwave and Flash. Careers that focus on user interface typically require bachelor's or master's degrees in Web design or architecture. Psychology courses or degrees are also helpful for those who would like to rise to the highest levels because they help developers understand how users interface with websites.

A Rocky Road?

As with many computer careers, predictions on the outlook for Web developers vary. The Bureau of Labor Statistics expects jobs relating to the Internet to be among the fastest growing through 2010. However, because of a slump in the economy at the turn of the century that caused many small companies to go out of business and large companies to lay off workers, many Web developers lost their jobs. Nevertheless, industry observers remain optimistic, including the company WetFeet, a publisher of online career guides, which writes: "While this career path has taken a beating lately, with people in the field being laid off by the thousands, as the Web grows over time (and it surely will), so will opportunities for designing websites."[73] WetFeet suggests that new technology, such as broadband, which facilitates the inclusion of video and audio on websites, will create new opportunities for people who keep updating their skills. In addition to new technologies as a source of job growth, the spending habits of Americans mean opportunities to create websites that facilitate e-commerce, a business that many observers expect to grow to $100 billion a year by 2005.

Experience Pays

Changes in the economy and the job outlook will undoubtedly affect the earnings of Web developers. However, a 2003 WetFeet report shows that programmers in this field earn $40,000 to

Internet jobs are expected to grow in the twenty-first century, and Web designers with experience will command the highest salaries.

$90,000 per year, editors $35,000 to $90,000, writers $30,000 to $75,000, and designers $35,000 to $75,000. The highest salaries in the Web development field are paid to those with proven skills gained through experience. In addition, working in a large city or with a big company can boost earnings. Organizations that provide certification, such as the World Organization of Webmasters, assert that completing their courses and exams and becoming certified increases earnings potential.

Challenges and Satisfaction

As noted earlier, Web developers face various technological challenges and may often find themselves working long and odd hours. Like programmers, Web developers also may suffer from physical ailments that result from many hours spent in front of a computer. These include eye strain, back pain, and carpal tunnel syndrome (pain in one or both wrists that may require surgery).

In spite of these drawbacks, Web developers have many reasons to feel satisfied with their work. For instance, they provide a service that benefits not only their clients but also the masses of people hungry for information and products that can be found on the Internet. Thus, Web developers find satisfaction in providing vital information and entertainment to a huge audience of users and in enabling companies to do business with unprecedented speed and efficiency. Like others in the field of computer technology, Web developers of the twenty-first century thrive because they work on the cutting edge of technological advances Americans have come to rely on in their everyday lives.

Notes

Introduction: A Definite Yet Unpredictable Future

1. Jesse Liberty, *The Complete Idiot's Guide to a Career in Computer Programming*. Indianapolis, IN: Que, 1999, p. 28.

2. Quoted in Dr. Allan Hoffman, "Tech Outlook 2003, Hiring and Spending Trends," Monster Technology, 2003. http://technology.monster.com.

3. Chris Stephenson and George Milbrandt, "Helping Students Prepare for Careers in Computing." *Learning and Leading with Technology*, December 2001, pp. 32–36.

4. Kim R. Wells, "Choosing Between Large and Small Companies," *Graduating Engineer and Computer Careers Online*, 2003. www.graduatingengineer.com.

Chapter 1: Computer Programmers

5. *Graduating Engineer and Computer Careers Online*, "Career Profiles, Computer Programming," 2003. www.graduatingengineer.com.

6. Max Gardner, e-mail interview with the author, July 2003.

7. Herbert Schildt, *C: The Complete Reference*, 3rd ed. Berkeley, CA: Osborne McGraw-Hill, 1995, p. 710.

8. Gardner, e-mail interview with the author.

9. Leon Atkinson, *Core PHP Programming*. Upper Saddle River, NJ: Prentice-Hall, 2004, p. 17.

10. Gardner, e-mail interview with the author.

11. Gardner, e-mail interview with the author.

12. Gardner, e-mail interview with the author.

13. Liberty, *The Complete Idiot's Guide to a Career in Computer Programming*, p. 156.

14. Quoted in *Graduating Engineer and Computer Careers Online*, "Career Profiles, Computer Programmers," www.graduatingengineer.com.

15. Daniel Kohanski, *The Philosophical Programmer, Reflections*

on the Moth in the Machine. New York: St. Martin's, 1998, p. 15.

16. Schildt, C: *The Complete Reference*, p. 713.

17. Quoted in David Robinson, "Good Listener: Dimitri Kanevsky Is Deaf, Yet His Software Helps Computers Hear and Transcribe Human Speech," *Time*, September 2, 2002, p. A25.

18. William A. Schaffer, *High-Tech Careers for Low-Tech People*. 2nd ed. Berkeley, CA: Ten Speed, 1999, p. 172.

19. Gardner, e-mail interview with the author.

20. Andrew Carter, "All About IT Certification," WetFeet, 2003. www.wetfeet.com.

21. Gardner, e-mail interview with the author.

Chapter 2: Network Administrators

22. Paul Della Maggiora and Jim Doherty, *Cisco Networking Simplified*. Indianapolis, IN: Cisco, 2003, p. 161.

23. *Communications News*, "Latest Network Management Products," April 2001, p. 74.

24. Della Maggiora and Doherty, *Cisco Networking Simplified*, p. 162.

25. Drew Bird and Mike Harwood, *Information Technology Careers: The Hottest Jobs for the New Millennium*. Scottsdale, AZ: Coriolis, 2000, p. 104.

26. Vincent Mase, telephone interview with the author, Del Mar, CA, September 2003.

27. Lou Dolinar, "Computer Worm Gives Scare to Network Administrators, Security Professionals," *Newsday*, August 23, 2003.

28. Alex Salkever, "As the Worm Turns: Lessons from Blaster," *BusinesWeek online*, August 21, 2003. www.business week.com.

29. Marc Spiwak, "Slow Web Performance? Step on the Accelerator," *Computer Reseller News*, August 4, 2003.

30. David Strom, "Self-Updating Router Firmware Creates

Problems," *InternetWeek*, July 1, 2003. www.internetweek. com.

31. Mase, telephone interview with the author.

32. Mase, telephone interview with the author.

33. ICCP-Institute for Certification of Computing Professionals, "Certified Computing Professional," 2001/2002. www.iccp.org.

34. Quoted in *Computer Weekly*, September 9, 2003, p. 2001.

35. Mase, telephone interview with the author.

36. Olivia Crosby, "New and Emerging Occupations," *Occupational Outlook Quarterly*, Fall 2002, p. 17.

Chapter 3: Hardware Engineers

37. Lowell Thing, ed., *The whatis?com Encyclopedia of Technology Terms*. Indianapolis, IN: Que, 2002, p. 308.

38. Julie Kling Burns, *Opportunities in Computer Careers*. Chicago: VGM, 2002, p. 8.

39. Roger Moncarz, "Computer Engineers," *Occupational Outlook Quarterly*, Fall 2000, p. 28.

40. Quoted in *Graduating Engineer and Computer Careers Online*, "Career Profiles, Hardware Engineering," 2003. www.graduatingengineer.com.

41. Bill Schweber, "Project-Coordination Tools: Get Your Act Together Before You Take It on the Road," *EDN Europe*, November 2001, pp.40–44.

42. Quoted in *Graduating Engineer and Computer Careers Online*, "Career Profiles, Software Engineering," 2003.

43. Patricia Daukantas, "Future PCs Could Run at Light Speed," *Government Computer News*, June 2, 2003, p. 27.

44. David Talbot, "Rolf Isermann, Mechatronics," *Technology Review*, February 2003, p. 40.

45. Adam Martin, "2003 Employment Outlook, Hardware, Short Circuit," *Business2.0*, March 2003. www.business2.com.

Chapter 4: Video Game Designers

46. Susan Lammers, *Programmers at Work, Interviews with 19 Programmers Who Shaped the Computer Industry*. Redmond, WA: Tempus Books of Microsoft Press, 1989, p. 265.

47. Quoted in *XBN*, "Return from Darkness," October/November 2003, p. 103.

48. Quoted in *Graduating Engineer and Computer Careers Online*, "Career Profiles, Questions with Software Engineers," 2003. www.graduatingengineer.com.

49. Bob Rafei, "Animating for Games . . . Naughty Dog Style," *Animation World Magazine*, February 28, 2003. http://mag.awn.com.

50. Quoted in Christopher Harz, "Small Screen, Big Possibilities," *Animation World Magazine*, July 31, 2003. http://mag.awn.com.

51. Quoted in Andrew Vestal and Che Chou, "Real Live Fantasies," *XBN*, October/November 2003, p. 48.

52. Quoted in George Jones, "Bye-Bye Blizzard," *Computer Gaming World*, October 2003, p. 43.

53. Michael Morrison, *Sams Teach Yourself Game Programming in 24 Hours*, Indianapolis, IN: Sams, 2003, p. 10.

54. Quoted in International Game Developers Association, "Breaking In, Preparing for Your Career in Games, Darryl S. Duncan." www.igda.org.

55. Morrison, *Sams Teach Yourself Game Programming in 24 Hours*, p. 12.

56. CoolGameJobs.com, "General Information." www.coolgamejobs.com.

57. Khanh T.L. Tran, "Need for New Games Spurs a Hiring Boom," *CareerJournal.com*. www.careerjournal.com.

Chapter 5: Computer Technicians

58. Harry Henderson, *Career Opportunities in Computers and Cyberspace*. New York: Checkmark, 1999, p. 52.

59. Jean Andrews, *Upgrade and Repair with Jean Andrews*.

Boston: Premier, 2003, p. 557.

60. Quoted in *Exploring Tech Careers: Real People Tell You What You Need to Know*, vol. 1. Chicago: Ferguson, 2001, p. 181.

61. Andrews, *Upgrade and Repair with Jean Andrews*, p. 559.

62. Andrews, *Upgrade and Repair with Jean Andrews*, p. 1, 122.

63. International Society of Certified Electronics Technicians, "About ISCET." www.iscet.org.

64. Olivia Crosby, "Associate Degree: Two Years to a Career or a Jump Start to a Bachelor's Degree," *Occupational Outlook Quarterly*, Winter 2002/2003, p. 4.

65. Bureau of Labor Statistics, U.S. Department of Labor, "Computer, Automated Teller, and Office Machine Repairers," *Occupational Outlook Handbook*, 2002–2003 ed. www.bls.gov.

66. Andrew Alpert and Jill Auyer, "The 1988–2000 Employment Projections: How Accurate Were They?" *Occupational Outlook Quarterly*, Spring 2003, p. 5.

Chapter 6: Web Developers

67. World Organization of Webmasters, "WOW Learning Center: Design and Usability." www.joinwow.org.

68. Emily Vander Veer et al., *Creating Web Pages All-in-One Desk Reference for Dummies*. Indianapolis, IN: Wiley, 2002, p. 119.

69. Jennifer Niederst, *Web Design in a Nutshell, a Desktop Quick Reference*. Sebastopol, CA: O'Reilly, p. 3.

70. Vander Veer et al, *Creating Web Pages All-in-One Desk Reference for Dummies*, p. 669.

71. Niederst, *Web Design in a Nutshell, a Desktop Quick Reference*, p. 330.

72. Schaffer, *High-Tech Careers for Low-Tech People*, p. 78.

73. WetFeet, "Web Design, Career Overview," 2003. www. wetfeet.com.

Organizations to Contact

Association for Computing Machinery (ACM)
1515 Broadway
New York, NY 10036
(212) 626-0500
website: www.acm.org

The first computer society, founded in 1947, promotes the advancement of information technology through publications, meetings, implementation of ethical standards for its members, and participation in the development of public policy. Conducts the prestigious International Collegiate Programming Contest.

IEEE Computer Society
1730 Massachusetts Ave. NW
Washington, DC 20036-1992
(202) 371-0101
http://computer.org

Part of the Institute of Electrical and Electronics Engineers, Inc., this society brings together computing professionals through chapter meetings and symposia. Develops standards for the computer industry and publishes *Computer* magazine.

Information Technology Association of America
1401 Wilson Blvd., Suite 1100
Arlington, VA 22209
(703) 522-5055
website: www.itaa.org

Trade association that promotes the interests of the information technology industry and the best use of technology in society through lobbying, collecting and publishing data about trends in the industry, and sponsoring educational and networking programs and meetings.

Institute for Certification of Computing Professionals (ICCP)
2350 East Devon Ave., Suite 115

Des Plaines, IL 60018
(800) 843-8227
website: www.iccp.org

Offers certification in many computer specialties including programming and network administration. The ICCP Education Foundation focuses on research and education.

Institute for Women and Technology
1501 Page Mill Rd., ms 1105
Palo Alto, CA 94304
(650) 236-4756
website: www.iwt.org
e-mail: info@iwt.org

Works to increase the impact of women in technology through sponsorship of the largest technical conference for women, and the "Systers" online community for women in computing. Conducts summit meetings with leading women in technology.

International Game Developers Association (IGDA)
600 Harrison St.
San Francisco, CA 94107
(415) 947-6235
website: www.igda.org
e-mail: info@igda.org

Publishes *Game Developer* magazine and provides networking and educational opportunities to members through participation in or sponsoring of international, national, and local events. Provides information on how to break into the field, support for students including scholarships to the international Game Developers Conference, and sponsors the Game Developers Choice Awards.

World Organization of Webmasters
9580 Oak Avenue Pkwy., Suite 7-177
Folsom, CA 95630
(916) 608-1597
website: www.joinwow.org
e-mail: info@joinwow.org

A nonprofit professional association that provides education and networking opportunities for Web professionals. Offers certification for beginning and advanced webmasters, Web designers, Web developers, and Web administrators.

For Further Reading

Books

Tonya Buell, *Cool Careers Without College for Web Surfers*. New York: Rosen, 2002. Good summaries of Web-related jobs that do not require college degrees, including webmaster, online instructor and researcher, day trader, and travel agent.

Careers in Focus, Internet. Chicago: Ferguson, 2001. Fun-to-read accounts of jobs relating to the Internet, including webmaster, online journalist, and video game designer.

Alan Freedman, *The Computer Glossary: The Complete Illustrated Dictionary*, 9th ed. Point Pleasant, PA: Computer Language, 2001. Over six thousand terms explained. Includes illustrations and multimedia CD-ROM.

Michael Fulton, *Exploring Careers in Cyberspace*. New York: Rosen, 1998. The author gives an insider look at jobs such as programming and Web design by interviewing people who perform those jobs.

Ceel Pasternak and Linda Thornburg, *Cool Careers for Girls*. Manassas Park, VA: Impact, 1999. Short portraits of women who have succeeded in a range of computing careers, with good graphics that call out technical definitions and personal qualities needed.

Linda B. Stair, *Careers in Computers*. Lincolnwood, IL: VGM, 2000. Good explanation of the link between various computer careers plus details about work within those careers.

U.S. Department of Labor, *Occupational Outlook Handbook, 2002–2003*. Washington, DC: Bureau of Labor Statistics, 2002. A primary sourcebook for career information. Includes up-to-date summaries of more than two hundred careers, with information on job duties, outlook, required training and education, and salaries.

John Vacca, *Computer Crime Scene Investigation*. Hingham, MA: Charles River, 2002. A comprehensive review of the need for, functions of, and tools used by computer forensic experts.

Websites

America's Career InfoNet (www.acinet.org). Government-sponsored website that contains massive amounts of easy-to-access information about careers, education, wages, and employers. Includes links to fifty-five hundred online career sources and has 360 career-specific videos for downloading.

Animation World Magazine (http://mag.awn.com). A fascinating exploration of the business, craft, and trends of computer and video animation.

Works Consulted

Books

Jean Andrews, *Upgrade and Repair with Jean Andrews*. Boston: Premier, 2003. A massive volume that contains not only highly technical information about repairing computers, but also helpful illustrated descriptions of how computers are made and work.

Leon Atkinson, *Core PHP Programming*. Upper Saddle River, NJ: Prentice-Hall, 2004. Highly technical discussion of how to use the PHP programming language.

Charles W. Berry and William H. Hawn Jr., *Computer and Internet Dictionary for Ages 9 to 99*. Hauppauge, NY: Barron's, 2001. An illustrated, easy-to-read dictionary. Includes a history of computers.

Drew Bird and Mike Harwood, *Information Technology Careers: The Hottest Jobs for the New Millennium*. Scottsdale, AZ: Coriolis, 2000. In-depth, well-organized look at the real work of information technology workers for more mature readers.

Julie Kling Burns, *Opportunities in Computer Careers*. Chicago: VGM, 2002. Brief descriptions of careers with an in-depth discussion of how to prepare for and find jobs.

Paul Della Maggiora and Jim Doherty, *Cisco Networking Simplified*. Indianapolis, IN: Cisco, 2003. Practical, illustrated instruction manual that describes the many components of creating networks using the Cisco system.

Exploring Tech Careers: Real People Tell You What You Need to Know, vol. 1. Chicago: Ferguson, 2001. An excellent reference with good descriptions of careers illustrated with real-life experiences.

50 Cutting Edge Jobs. Chicago: Ferguson, 2000. Brings to life the newest jobs of the twenty-first century, including computer technology jobs such as Web producer and computer animator.

Michael T. Goodrich, Roberto Tamassia, and David Mount, *Data Structures and Algorithms in C++*. Wiley, 2004. Technical handbook on the language C++.

Harry Henderson, *Career Opportunities in Computers and Cyberspace*. New York: Checkmark, 1999. Summaries of a broad range of careers, including salary, education, and advancement information.

James J. Hobuss, *Building Sybase Web Sites*. Upper Saddle River, NJ: Prentice-Hall, 1998. A technical manual on creating database applications for the Web.

Daniel Kohanski, *The Philosophical Programmer, Reflections on the Moth in the Machine*. New York: St. Martin's, 1998. Thought-provoking essays on the intellectual and ethical nature of programming.

Susan Lammers, *Programmers at Work, Interviews with 19 Programmers Who Shaped the Computer Industry*. Redmond, WA: Tempus Books of Microsoft Press, 1989. Fascinating interviews with programmers who paved the way for twenty-first century programming.

Jesse Liberty, *The Complete Idiot's Guide to a Career in Computer Programming*. Indianapolis, IN: Que, 1999. An easy-to-follow introduction to programming careers.

Michael Morrison, *Sams Teach Yourself Game Programming in 24 Hours*. Indianapolis, IN: Sams, 2003. An easy-to-understand technical guide to teach individuals with programming experience how to create computer games on a home computer.

Jennifer Niederst, *Web Design in a Nutshell, a Desktop Quick Reference*. Sebastopol, CA: O'Reilly, 1999. A technical discussion of designing sites.

William A. Schaffer, *High-Tech Careers for Low-Tech People*. 2nd ed. Berkeley, CA: Ten Speed, 1999. A pleasantly informative discussion of options for people without advanced technical skills.

Herbert Schildt, *C: The Complete Reference*, 3rd ed. Berkeley, CA: Osborne McGraw-Hill, 1995. Highly technical discussion of the computer language, C.

Lowell Thing, ed., *The whatis?com Encyclopedia of Technology Terms*. Indianapolis, IN: Que, 2002. A helpful encyclopedia of computer-related terms.

Emily Vander Veer et al., *Creating Web Pages All-in-One Desk Reference for Dummies*. Indianapolis, IN: Wiley, 2002. An outstanding reference work organized in a series of books with separate indexes. The cover the basics, Web programs, and how to publish a website.

Periodicals

Andrew Alpert and Jill Auyer, "The 1988–2000 Employment Projections: How Accurate Were They?" *Occupational Outlook Quarterly*, Spring 2003.

Calvin Bruce, "Information Technology, a Booming Career Now and into the Future," *Black Collegian*, October 1999.

Michael Castelluccio, "Revolutionary? Not Really," *Strategic Finance*, February 2003.

Communications News, "Latest Network Management Products," April 2001.

Computer Weekly, September 9, 2003.

Olivia Crosby, "Associate Degree: Two Years to a Career or a Jump Start to a Bachelor's Degree," *Occupational Outlook Quarterly*, Winter 2002/2003.

———, "New and Emerging Occupations," *Occupational Outlook Quarterly*, Fall 2002.

Patricia Daukantas, "Future PCs Could Run at Light Speed," *Government Computer News*, June 2, 2003.

Lou Dolinar, "Computer Worm Gives Scare to Network Administrators, Security Professionals," *Newsday*, August 23, 2003.

eWeek, "The New Tech Apprentice," June 10, 2002.

K. Oanh Ha, "Race, Gender Not Issues for IBM Female Software Engineer," *Knight Ridder/Tribune Business News*, February 20, 2003.

George Jones, "Bye-Bye Blizzard," *Computer Gaming World*, October 2003.

Erika Jonietz, "Nancy Lynch & Stephen Garland, Software Assurance," *Technology Review*, February 2003.

Bill Kovacs, "The Play's the Thing, but . . . ," *Computer Graphics World*, August 2003.

Jim Leeke, "Humane Technology: Teaching the Techies to Talk," *PC Week*, July 21, 1987.

Roger Moncarz, "Computer Engineers," *Occupational Outlook Quarterly*, Fall 2000.

David Robinson, "Good Listener: Dimitri Kanevsky Is Deaf, Yet His Software Helps Computers Hear and Transcribe Human Speech," *Time*, September 2, 2002.

Bill Schweber, "Project-Coordination Tools: Get Your Act Together Before You Take It on the Road," *EDN Europe*, November 2001.

Evan Shamoon, "Here Come the Xbots . . .," *XBN*, October/November 2003.

Marc Spiwak, "Slow Web Performance? Step on the Accelerator," *Computer Reseller News*, August 4, 2003.

Chris Stephenson and George Milbrandt, "Helping Students Prepare for Careers in Computing," *Learning & Leading with Technology*, December 2001.

David Talbot, "Rolf Isermann, Mechatronics," *Technology Review*, February 2003.

Andrew Vestal and Che Chou, "Real Live Fantasies," *XBN*, October/November 2003.

XBN, "Return from Darkness," October/November 2003.

Internet Sources

Michele Bitoun Blecher, "Minority Issues, a Second Chance," *Graduating Engineer and Computer Careers Online*, 2003. www.graduatingengineer.com.

Bureau of Labor Statistics, U.S. Department of Labor, "Computer, Automated Teller, and Office Machine Repairers," *Occupational Outlook Handbook*, 2002–2003 ed. www.bls.gov.

Andrew Carter, "All About IT Certification," WetFeet 2003. www.wetfeet.com.

CoolGameJobs.com, "General Information." www.coolgamejobs. com.

Graduating Engineer Computing Careers Online, "Career Profiles, Computer Programmers," 2002. www.graduatingengineer.com.

————, "Career Profiles, Computer Programming," 2003.

————, "Career Profiles, Hardware Engineering," 2003.

————, "Career Profiles, Questions with with Software Engineers," 2003.

————, "Career Profiles, Software Engineering," 2003.

————, "Career Profiles, Software Engineering, part 2," 2003.

Christopher Harz, "Small Screen, Big Possibilities," *Animation World Magazine*, July 31, 2003. http://mag.awn.com.

Allan Hoffman, "Tech Outlook 2003, Hiring and Spending Trends," Monster Technology. http://technology.monster.com.

ICCP-Institure for Certification of Computing Professionals, "Certified Computing Professional," 2001/2002. www.iccp.org.

International Game Developers Association, "Breaking In, Preparing for Your Career in Games, Darryl S. Duncan." www.igda.org.

International Society of Certified Electronics Technicians, "About ISCET." www.iscet.org.

Adam Martin, "2003 Employment Outlook, Hardware, Short Circuit," *Business2.0*, March 2003. www.business2.com.

Bob Rafei, "Animating for Games . . . Naughty Dog Style," *Animation World Magazine*, February 28, 2003. http://mag.awn.com.

Alex Salkever, "As the Worm Turns: Lessons from Blaster," *BusinessWeek online*, August 21, 2003. www.businessweek.com.

David Strom, "Self-Updating Router Firmware Creates Problems," *InternetWeek*, July 1, 2003, www.internetweek.com.

Khanh T.L. Tran, "Need for New Games Spurs a Hiring Boom," *CareerJournal.com*. www.careerjournal.com.

Kim R. Wells, "Choosing Between Large and Small Companies," *Graduating Engineer and Computer Careers Online*, 2003. www.graduatingengineer.com.

WetFeet, "Web Design, Career Overview," 2003. www.wetfeet.com.

World Organization of Webmasters, "WOW Learning Center: Design and Usability." www.joinwow.org.

Pamphlets

Congressional Commission on the Advancement of Women and Minorities in Science, Engineering and Technology Development, "Land of Plenty, Diversity as America's Competitive Edge in Science, Engineering and Technology," September 2000.

Federal Trade Commission, Direct Marketing Association, and Internet Alliance, *How to Comply with the Children's Online Privacy Protection Act, a Guide from the Federal Trade Commission, the Direct Marketing Association, and the Internet Alliance.*

Index

Picture Credits

About the Author

Patrice Cassedy is the author of Lucent's *Understanding Flowers for Algernon* and *Teen Pregnancy* as well as several of the publisher's career books, including *Biotechnology*, *Education*, and *Finance*. Before publishing her first book, Cassedy wrote many articles on subjects including the craft of writing and family safety. She worked nearly twenty years as a lawyer for financial institutions, taught law school, and completed courses in marketing and retailing. She enjoys her latest passion, house design and interior decorating. She also enjoys guiding young people as they discover their career ambitions, especially her daughter Eva, who is interested in becoming a doctor or psychologist, and her son Michael, who is a jazz pianist living in New York.